Reading STREET

Grades K-2

Scott Foresman

Vocabulary

Teacher's Guide and Student Worktext

PEARSON

Glenview, Illinois
Boston, Massachusetts
Chandler, Arizona
Upper Saddle River, New Jersey

D1511706

ISBN-13: 978-0-328-47832-3
ISBN-10:   0-328-47832-6
1 2 3 4 5 6 7 8 9 10 V084 18 17 16 15 14 13 12 11 10 09

Reading Street Response to Intervention Kit

Program Overview

The *Reading Street Response to Intervention Kit* provides targeted instruction in core English-Language Arts standards for Grades K to 2 in each of the five critical areas of reading instruction: phonemic awareness, phonics and decoding, fluency, vocabulary, and comprehension. The Kit, designed for small-group or one-on-one instruction, includes lessons on core skills, allowing teachers to focus on the skills children need most and help them make rapid progress to achieve grade-level proficiency.

Each lesson includes three customized mini-lessons differentiated for the following reading and skill levels:

Mini-Lesson 1: Level 1 (pre-K to K)

Mini-Lesson 2: Level 2 (K to Grade 1)

Mini-Lesson 3: Level 3 (Grades 1 to 2)

For additional information about the *Reading Street Response to Intervention Kit*, see "How to Use This Kit" in the RTI Implementation Guide.

Vocabulary Teacher's Guide and Student Worktext

The Teacher's Guide portion includes

- three-tiered, differentiated lessons for 20–25 core skills and strategies
- a routine, activities, and 16–20 word lists for teaching high-frequency words
- reinforcement for the strategies and routines used in the core program
- vocabulary strategies embedded in each vocabulary skill lesson

The Student Worktext portion includes

- additional skills practice
- word cards and context sentences
- School+Home activities on every page

Lesson Features

- **Set the scene** introduces the lesson topic to children.
- **Objectives** identifies the instructional objectives for children.
- **Materials** lists the Worktext components and additional supporting materials for the lesson.
- **Direct teaching** is provided through explicit teacher modeling and consistent routines.
- **Mini-Lessons** are provided for differentiated instruction.
- **Guided practice** for each mini-lesson consists of ample group practice with multiple response opportunities.
- **Independent practice (On Their Own)** allows children to apply skills independently.
- **If…/then…** provides teachers with specific activities for reinforcing skills.

Table of Contents Vocabulary

Vocabulary
Teacher's Guide

Vocabulary Lesson 1
High-Frequency Words

Objectives:

- Learn the correct spellings and pronunciations of high-frequency words.
- Use and recognize high-frequency words in sentences.

MATERIALS

Worktext pp. 2–33
Routine Cards 1, 8

WORD LIST 1

come	said
help	what
little	where
many	your

Set the scene Remind children that putting letters together makes words. We learn to read some words by saying the sounds that the letters spell. Other words we have to learn by just remembering the letters. Today we're going to learn words by remembering their letters.

Model and teach Write the words *many, come,* and *said.* These are words that I need to remember the letters for. To help me remember the words, I will say the words and spell them. This word is *many.* It has four letters. **Point to the letters as appropriate.** The word *many* is spelled *m, a, n, y.* Using the word in a sentence helps me understand it: *I have many friends at school.*

Point to the word *come.* This word is *come.* It has four letters: *c, o, m, e.* A sentence with this word is *I wish you could come to my party.*

Then point to the word *said.* The word *said* is spelled *s, a, i, d.* A sentence with this word is *May said to have another cookie.*

1 Introduce the Words

Routine   Nondecodable Words

1 Say and Spell   Some words we learn by remembering the letters rather than saying the sounds. We will say and spell the words to learn them. Write the word *your.* This is the word *your.* The letters in *your* are *y-o-u-r, your.* What are the letters in *your*? Have children say and spell the word, first with you and then without you.

2 Demonstrate Meaning   Tell me a sentence using this word.

If... children have trouble using the word in a sentence,
then... identify the word and model how to use it in a sentence: The word is *your.* A sentence with *your* is *I like your hat.* Have children repeat the sentence.

3 Write   Point to the word *your.* Now you write *your.* What letters are in *your*? Have children confirm their spelling by comparing it to what you've written.

If... children have difficulty writing the word,
then... point to each letter in the word, name it, and allow time for children to write it.

Repeat this routine with the remaining words in the Word List.

2 Read Words

Guide Practice Now we will read sentences that have today's words in them. Distribute photocopies of worktext p. 3. Read aloud the first word on Worktext p. 3 and its sentence on Worktext p. 2. Have children follow along in their books and point to each word in the sentence as you read. Then ask children to repeat the sentence after you.

Point to the first word. What's the word? Allow three seconds for children to identify each word before they read it aloud. For decodable words, remind children to blend the sounds. Continue in this way with each word.

Second Reading Have children read the whole sentence at a natural pace as they point to each word. Have children cut apart the cards and keep them for word reading practice.

If... children cannot read a word,
then... model how to say and spell the high-frequency words (Routine Card 8) and use sound-by-sound blending (Routine Card 1) for decodable words.

3 More Practice

On Their Own Use Activity 1 on p. T•9 for more practice with the lesson's high-frequency words. After the group has successfully completed the activity, point to the words in random order and ask individuals to read them. Then ask children to find the word within its sentence on p. 2 of the Worktext. Finally, have children create their own sentences that include the word.

High-Frequency Word Activities

Activity 1

Find the missing word   Give each child a set of high-frequency word cards. Say sentences that are missing one of the high-frequency words. Have children hold up the missing words, say and spell them, and then as a group repeat the completed sentence. For additional practice, ask children to come up with their own sentences that are missing one of the high-frequency words. As a class or in small groups, ask children to find the missing words for one another's sentences.

Activity 2

Write a word   Have children work in pairs. Give each pair a set of word cards, a book, pencils, and paper. Have pairs set up the book between them as a barrier. Partner A picks a word card and spells the word, one letter at a time. Partner B writes the letters. When the word has been spelled, Partner B reads the word. Then partners switch roles. For additional practice, ask students to use the words in sentences.

Activity 3

Word Bingo   Create a simple Bingo Card with nine boxes, three down and three across. For each child, write the high-frequency words in random order on copies of the Bingo Card. If there are fewer than nine words, designate extra spaces as "free" spaces. Say a high-frequency word. Have children find the word on their cards and place a marker on it. When children get Bingo, have them read all the winning words aloud. Continue playing the game until multiple children get Bingo and say their winning words aloud. At the end of each game, invite remaining children to say which words on their boards had not yet been called.

Activity 4

Guess the Word   Give each child a set of high-frequency word cards, pencils, and paper. Ask each child to number the paper 1–5. Then give children five clues relating to a high-frequency word from the set. Clues can include the first letter of the word, the number of letters in the word, a rhyming word, a definition, or a sentence that includes the word. After the first clue, allow children time to look through their high-frequency word cards. Ask them to silently guess which high-frequency word you are talking about. Children should write their guess next to the number 1 on their paper. Follow the same procedure for the remaining four clues. If later clues confirm a child's original guess, he or she will write the same word multiple times.

WORD LIST 2

could	people
food	there
live	together
paper	work

To introduce and practice the words in Word List 2, use:
- Lesson 1, pp. T•7–T•8
- Worktext, pp. 4–5
    - **p. 4** Context Sentences
    - **p. 5** Word Cards
- Activity 2, p. T•9

WORD LIST 3

always	grow
around	their
become	water
family	were

To introduce and practice the words in Word List 3, use:
- Lesson 1, pp. T•7–T•8
- Worktext, pp. 6–7
    - **p. 6** Context Sentences
    - **p. 7** Word Cards
- Activity 3, p. T•9

WORD LIST 4

enough	nothing
every	our
everything	own
house	school

To introduce and practice the words in Word List 4, use:
- Lesson 1, pp. T•7–T•8
- Worktext, pp. 8–9
    - **p. 8** Context Sentences
    - **p. 9** Word Cards
- Activity 4, p. T•9

WORD LIST 5

afraid	friends
again	goodbye
does	know
done	read

To introduce and practice the words in Word List 5, use:
- Lesson 1, pp. T•7–T•8
- Worktext, pp. 10–11
    - **p. 10** Context Sentences
    - **p. 11** Word Cards
- Activity 1, p. T•9

WORD LIST 6

about	surprise
before	won't
right	worry
sign	would

To introduce and practice the words in Word List 6, use:
- Lesson 1, pp. T•7–T•8
- Worktext, pp. 12–13
    - **p. 12** Context Sentences
    - **p. 13** Word Cards
- Activity 2, p. T•9

WORD LIST 7

above	great
colors	once
draw	pictures
found	touch

To introduce and practice the words in Word List 7, use:
- Lesson 1, pp. T•7–T•8
- Worktext, pp. 14–15
    - **p. 14** Context Sentences
    - **p. 15** Word Cards
- Activity 3, p. T•9

WORD LIST 8

across	opened
because	remember
laugh	thought
only	took

To introduce and practice the words in Word List 8, use:
- Lesson 1, pp. T•7–T•8
- Worktext, pp. 16–17
    - **p. 16** Context Sentences
    - **p. 17** Word Cards
- Activity 4, p. T•9

WORD LIST 9

among	toward
behind	instead
door	loved
eyes	shoes

To introduce and practice the words in Word List 9, use:
- Lesson 1, pp. T•7–T•8
- Worktext, pp. 18–19
    - **p. 18** Context Sentences
    - **p. 19** Word Cards
- Activity 1, p. T•9

WORD LIST 10

against	heavy
another	none
early	should
goes	today

To introduce and practice the words in Word List 10, use:
- Lesson 1, pp. T•7–T•8
- Worktext, pp. 20–21
  - **p. 20** Context Sentences
  - **p. 21** Word Cards
- Activity 2, p. T•9

WORD LIST 11

answered	different
beautiful	learn
built	science
country	through

To introduce and practice the words in Word List 11, use:
- Lesson 1, pp. T•7–T•8
- Worktext, pp. 22–23
  - **p. 22** Context Sentences
  - **p. 23** Word Cards
- Activity 3, p. T•9

WORD LIST 12

build	move
couldn't	someone
everywhere	somewhere
machines	world

To introduce and practice the words in Word List 12, use:
- Lesson 1, pp. T•7–T•8
- Worktext, pp. 24–25
  - **p. 24** Context Sentences
  - **p. 25** Word Cards
- Activity 4, p. T•9

WORD LIST 13

animals	listen
break	often
gone	pieces
heard	though

To introduce and practice the words in Word List 13, use:
- Lesson 1, pp. T•7–T•8
- Worktext, pp. 26–27
  - **p. 26** Context Sentences
  - **p. 27** Word Cards
- Activity 1, p. T•9

WORD LIST 14

bought	minute
brought	whole
either	worst
everybody	you're

To introduce and practice the words in Word List 14, use:
- Lesson 1, pp. T•7–T•8
- Worktext, pp. 28–29
    - **p. 28** Context Sentences
    - **p. 29** Word Cards
- Activity 2, p. T•9

WORD LIST 15

been	guess
believe	half
caught	neighbor
finally	tomorrow

To introduce and practice the words in Word List 15, use:
- Lesson 1, pp. T•7–T•8
- Worktext, pp. 30–31
    - **p. 30** Context Sentences
    - **p. 31** Word Cards
- Activity 3, p. T•9

WORD LIST 16

buy	money
clothes	question
daughters	taught
hours	youngest

To introduce and practice the words in Word List 16, use:
- Lesson 1, pp. T•7–T•8
- Worktext, pp. 32–33
    - **p. 32** Context Sentences
    - **p. 33** Word Cards
- Activity 4, p. T•9

Vocabulary Lesson 2
Classify and Categorize

Objectives:
- Classify pictures and words into groups.
- Identify categories within groups of words.

MATERIALS
Worktext pp. 34–36

Set the scene Introduce to children the concept of classifying. Classifying words helps us see how the words are alike. To *classify* means to group things that are the same in some way.

Model and teach Model for children how to classify words. When we classify, we will start with a group of words that have something in common. Then we will see what smaller groups we can make from the larger one. Write the words *peach, cheese, apple,* and *ice cream.* All of these are words for things we can eat. Now I am going to put these words into two smaller groups: *fruit* and *foods that come from milk.* Draw two columns on the board.

Then model for children how to look at each word to decide what category to put it in. I will start with the word *peach.* A peach does not come from milk. A peach grows on a tree. It is a kind of fruit. Write *peach* in the *fruit* column. Have children help you sort each of the remaining words into one of the columns.

If... children have difficulty understanding what it means to classify,
then... help them classify items in the classroom, such as "things we write with."

Remind children that...
- classifying means putting words into groups.
- big groups of words can be broken up into smaller groups.

Word List
animals	monkey
cat	pets
chicken	pig
farm	zebra
fish	zoo

Guide Practice
Show the pictures on Worktext p. 34 to children. I want to sort this big group of animals into three small groups. The first group is called *Zoo Animals.* These are wild animals that are kept in a zoo. The second group is called *Farm Animals,* which are animals that live on a farm. The third group is *Pets.* They are animals that live with you.

Have children help you sort the first picture into a group.
- Here is a picture of a chicken. Say the word with me: *chicken.*
- Where can you find a chicken? (on a farm)
- Could you find a chicken in a zoo or as someone's pet in a home? (not usually)
- What's the best group to put the chicken in? (farm animals)

If... children have difficulty understanding how the animals in the small groups are related,
then... point out that the animals are classified based on where they are normally found and brainstorm other zoo animals, farm animals, and pets.

On Their Own For additional practice classifying and categorizing, assign Worktext p. 34.

Mini-Lesson 2

Remind children that...
- classifying means putting words into groups.
- the same group of words can be classified in different ways.

Word List

boots	shorts
cap	ski hat
clothes	socks
jacket	sweater
pants	T-shirt

Guide Practice
Write *jacket, boots, socks, T-shirt, jeans,* and *shorts.* These words all name things to wear. A *sweater* is something I wear over my other clothes to keep warm. If it is cold or wet outside, I wear *boots* on my feet. Since *sweater* and *boots* have something in common,

I can group these words together. Let's think about other ways to group words for things that we wear.

- The first word I'm going to say is *jacket.* Say it with me: *jacket.*
- What is a jacket? (Possible responses: something you wear outside, something that keeps you warm, something with a zipper)
- What word do you think is like *jacket?* Why? (Possible responses: *sweater* because it's worn on the top half of the body; *boots* because they're worn outside)

Continue in this way with the remaining words.

If... children have difficulty sorting the words, **then...** ask them more questions to get them to understand each word.

On Their Own Ask children to complete Worktext p. 35.

Mini-Lesson 3

Remind children that...
- classifying means putting words into groups.
- the same group of words can be classified in different ways.

Word List

airplane	elephant
bicycle	helicopter
bus	sailboat
camel	scooter
canoe	train

Guide Practice
Today we're going to look at words that tell us ways we can get places. We're going to figure out how to put these words into groups. Write *airplane, scooter, canoe, bicycle, helicopter,* and *camel.* Read the words aloud. I know all these words can get me places. I start with the first word: *airplane.*

- What do you know about an airplane? (Possible responses: it flies, it runs using engines, it can transport many people.)
- What other words in this list go with *airplane?* (Possible response: helicopter) Why? (because *helicopter* and *plane* both name things that fly)

Continue in this way with the remaining words.

If... children have difficulty finding similarities, **then...** encourage them to think about what they know about each object.

On Their Own Assign Worktext p. 36 to children.

Vocabulary Lesson 3
Alphabetize

Objectives:

- Children understand what it means to alphabetize.
- Children can alphabetize words by the first letter.
- Children in higher levels can alphabetize words by the first and the second letter.

MATERIALS

Worktext pp. 37–39

Set the scene Introduce to children the concept of alphabetical order. We have talked about the alphabet. What are the first letters of the alphabet? (A, B, C) Sometimes it is helpful to put words in *ABC* order. This is also called *alphabetical order.*

Model and teach Model putting words into alphabetical order for children. To puts words in alphabetical order, I need to look at the first letter in each word. **Write the words** *ball* and *cake*. This is the word *ball*. I know that the first letter in the word *ball* is *b*. This is the word *cake*. I know that the first letter in the word *cake* is *c*. After looking at the first letter in each word, I think of the alphabet. Does the letter *b* come before or after the letter *c*? I know that *b* comes before *c*. That means that the word *ball* comes before the word *cake* in alphabetical order. **Rewrite the word** *ball* or *cake* so that the two words are in order.

After children understand how to put A, B, and C words in alphabetical order, introduce a word from later in the alphabet, such as *frog*, to the *ball* and *cake* list. Explain to children that a list of words in alphabetical order does not have to include a word that starts with each letter of the alphabet. If children are able, they can check their answers using a dictionary. Explain that a dictionary lists words in alphabetical order.

Mini-Lesson 1

Remind children that...

- *alphabetical,* or *ABC, order* means putting words in the same order as the alphabet.
- words are alphabetized by the first letter of each word.

Word List

and	car
apple	do
big	dog
bat	eat
can	egg

Guide Practice

Write *can, and, eat, do,* and *big*. Read each word and say its first letter: This is the word *can. Can* starts with the letter *c*. What is the first letter in the word *can?* Repeat for all five words. You may choose to underline the first letter in each word for emphasis.

To put words in ABC order means to put words in the same order as the alphabet. What are the first five letters of the alphabet? (A, B, C, D, E) Which word do you see that starts with the letter A? (*and*) What letter comes after A? (B) Do any of the words start with B? (*big*) Continue with the rest of the words. As children work through the words, rewrite them in alphabetical order.

If... children have difficulty organizing the words, **then...** write the letters A–E so children can see the connection between the alphabet and the first letters of each word.

On Their Own With children, name each picture on Worktext p. 37 and assign the page.

Mini-Lesson 2

Remind children that...

• *alphabetizing* means putting words in the order of the alphabet.
• words are alphabetized by the first letter of each word.

Word List

airplane	father
baby	kite
bee	moon
child	mother
cloud	sun

Guide Practice

Write the words *mother, father, baby,* and *child*. These are some words for members of a family. This is the word *mother.* The word *mother* starts with the letter *m*. Repeat for the remaining words.

Then guide children in alphabetizing the list. Let's look at the first two words in the list. What is the first letter of the word *mother*? (m) What is the first letter of the word *father*? (f) Does *f* come before *m* in the alphabet? Give children several moments to come up with an answer. Yes, *f* comes before *m* in the alphabet. In alphabetical order, the word *father* comes before the word *mother.* As you work with children through the rest of the list, rewrite the words in alphabetical order.

If... children have difficulty organizing the words, **then...** write the letters A–Z, and ask children to draw a line between the first letter of each word and its corresponding letter in the alphabet.

On Their Own With children, name each picture on Worktext p. 38 and assign the page.

Mini-Lesson 3

Remind children that...

• *alphabetizing* means putting words into the order of the alphabet.
• if two words start with the same letter, they can be alphabetized using the next letters in each word.

Word List

Friday	today
Monday	tomorrow
Saturday	Tuesday
Sunday	Wednesday
Thursday	yesterday

Guide Practice

When we want to alphabetize two words that start with the same letters, we need to look at the next letters in each word. When we find letters that are different, we can see which comes first in the alphabet. Let's

alphabetize the words *today, tomorrow,* and *yesterday.* Write the words and say them aloud.

• Which two words start with the same letter? (*today* and *tomorrow*)
• Look at the second letter in these words. Are they different? (no)
• Look at the third letter in these words. Are they different? (yes). The third letter in *today* is *d,* and the third letter in *tomorrow* is *m*.
• Does *d* come before or after *m* in the alphabet? (before)
• So which word comes first in alphabetical order: *today* or *tomorrow*? (*today*)

If... children have difficulty alphabetizing the words, **then...** cross out or cover up the ends of the words so children can focus on the beginning letters.

On Their Own With children, read through the days of the week listed on Worktext p. 39 and assign the page.

Vocabulary Lesson 4
Compound Words

Objectives:
- Understand how to read and recognize compound words.
- Use compound words correctly in sentences.

MATERIALS
Worktext pp. 40–42

Set the scene Introduce to children the concept of compound words. Today we are going to learn about words called *compound words*. A *compound word* is made of two small words. Looking at the small words can help us understand the meaning of the compound word.

Model and teach Model reading a compound word. Write *bedroom. Bedroom* is made up of two words: *bed* and *room*. A *bed* is something you sleep in. A *room* is a place with walls. A *bedroom* is a place you sleep in. It has a bed. This is how I read a compound word. First, I figure out the first word. **Cover** *room* and read *bed.* Then I read the second word. Then I read the two parts together. **Run your hand under the word parts as you read:** *bed, room, bedroom.* A sentence with *bedroom* is *I want to paint my bedroom blue.*

Follow the same procedure with the word *homework. Homework* means "work done at home." Use the word in a sentence: *Finish your homework before you go play.* For additional practice, ask children to name the two small words that make up *doorbell, snowball, goldfish,* or other compound words. Ask children to describe each word and use it in a sentence. If children know how to use a dictionary, explain that they can use it to look up the meaning of a compound word.

Mini-Lesson 1

Remind children that...
- a compound word is a word made of two words.
- breaking apart a compound word can help explain the word's meaning.

Word List

backpack	goldfish
baseball	playground
bedtime	raincoat
cupcake	rowboat
footprint	teapot

Guide Practice
Some words are made of two words put together. Let's think about the word *bedtime.* Ask children to repeat the word. Can you hear the two small words in the word *bedtime?* You might pause between *bed* and *time* as a hint. You know the word *bed.* A *bed* is a place where you sleep. *Time* is a part of the day. The time when you go

to sleep is called *bedtime.* What is a sentence with this word? (Possible response: My mom tells me when it is bedtime.)

Follow the same procedure with the words *cupcake, teapot, rowboat,* and *raincoat.* You may need to explain to children the meanings of the small words *tea* in *teapot* and *row* in *rowboat.*

If... children have difficulty using compound words in sentences,
then... give them examples: *I ate a chocolate cupcake; I see a rowboat on the river.*

On Their Own Help children identify each picture on Worktext p. 40 and assign the page.

Mini-Lesson 2

Remind children that...
- a compound word is a word made of two words.
- breaking apart a compound word can help explain the word's meaning.

Word List

bluebird	moonlight
bookstore	nutshell
campfire	popcorn
classroom	seashell
mailbox	toothbrush

Guide Practice

Write the words *bluebird, classroom,* and *bookstore.* This is the word *bluebird.* A *bluebird* is a bird that is the color blue. What is the first small word? Cover *bird* with your hand as a hint. What is the second small word? Cover *blue.* A sentence with the word *bluebird* is *A bluebird sits outside my window.* Repeat the process for *classroom.*

- What is the first small word in the word *classroom*? (*class*) What is the second small word? (*room*)
- What is a classroom? (a room that holds a class)
- Can you say sentence using this word? (Possible response: We sat in the classroom.)

Follow the same procedure for *bookstore, nutshell,* and *moonlight.*

If... children have difficulty connecting compounds words to small words,
then... define the compound words using the small words: A *bookstore* is a *store* that sells *books; Moonlight* is *light* from the *moon.*

On Their Own Assign Worktext p. 41 to children.

Mini-Lesson 3

Remind children that...
- a compound word is a word made of two words.
- breaking apart a compound word can help explain the word's meaning.

Word List

bathtub	haircut
birthday	lunchbox
bookshelf	newspaper
firefighter	skateboard
fireplace	snowman

Guide Practice

Write *birthday, lunchbox, firefighter,* and *haircut.* Have children read the words with you. Then as a group, identify the small words that make up each compound word. Have children tell the meaning of the word and use it in a sentence.

- What is the first compound word? (*birthday*)
- What is the first small word in the word birthday? (*birth*) That's right. A *birth* is when a baby is born.
- What is the second small word? (*day*) Yes. A *day* is part of a week.
- *Birthday* is a word that means what? (the day that someone is born)
- Can you say a sentence that uses this word? (Sample response: I had a party on my birthday.)

Repeat the process for *lunchbox, firefighter,* and *haircut.*

If... children cannot determine the small words that make up the compound word,
then... cover the second word and have children read the first word aloud and tell what it means. Reveal the second word in the same way.

On Their Own Assign Worktext p. 42 for practice.

Descriptive Words: Numbers and Color

Objectives:
- Learn vocabulary for numbers and colors.
- Use vocabulary to describe pictures and ideas.

MATERIALS
Worktext pp. 43–45

Set the scene

When we describe things, we paint pictures with words. One way to paint a picture with words is to say the number and the color of what you see. Is your bedroom painted bright orange or light blue? Can you see three stars in the sky or a hundred? Knowing words for numbers and colors will help you describe the things you see and use every day.

Model and teach

Point to your desk. This is a desk. The word *desk* tells me that someone sits here and works or studies. The word *desk* doesn't tell me much about the desk. If I want someone to see what I see, I have to use more words that tell about the desk. **Use the following description as a guide. Base your description on the desk children are viewing.** To paint my picture, I will ask myself questions. What does the desk look like? It is brown and blue. What is on the desk? Four yellow pencils and a green notebook are on the desk. What is special about the desk? It has two blue drawers.

If I say "I am sitting at a desk," you will picture a desk. It might not look much like this desk. If I say "I am sitting at a desk. The desk is brown and blue and has two blue drawers. There are four yellow pencils and a green notebook on the desk," then you will see a clearer picture of the desk I am telling you about.

Have children describe the classroom. Encourage them to use words for colors and numbers in their descriptions.

Remind children that...
- *describing* is painting a picture with words.
- we can use words for numbers and colors to describe.

Word List

black	red
blue	three
brown	two
four	white
one	yellow

Guide Practice
Write the words *one, two, three,* and *four* in a column. Write the words *red, blue, brown, yellow, black,* and *white* in a separate column. Point to the column with numbers. The words in this list are words for numbers. This is the number one. Say the word with me: *one.* Say the rest of the numbers aloud, and repeat the process for the colors column.

We can use number and color words to talk about things that we see or think about. Right now I am thinking about two yellow bananas. Point to the words *two* and *yellow.* Ask children to use words for colors and numbers to describe real or imaginary objects.

- What is something you can think of that is red? (Possible response: apples)
- Think about the apples. How many do you see? (Possible response: three)
- Tell me about the apples using the words we learned today. (There are three red apples.)

If... children have difficulty recognizing words for numbers and colors,

then... use the High-Frequency Word Activities on p. T•9.

On Their Own Read aloud the directions on Worktext p. 43 and assign the page.

Mini-Lesson 2

Remind children that...
- *describing* is painting a picture with words.
- we can use words for numbers and colors to describe.

Word List

color	many
dark	nine
eight	seven
five	six
light	ten

Guide Practice

Write the words *five, six, seven, eight, nine,* and *ten* in a column. The words in this list are words for numbers. Say each number aloud and ask children to repeat.

We can use number words to talk about things: *There are five people in my family.* If there is a lot of something, you can use the word *many* instead of using a number word.

Write *many* on the board. There are *many* flowers in my garden. Ask students to come up with sentences that include the numbers 5–10 or the word *many.*

We can also use color words to talk about things. What are some words for colors that you know? Then write *light* and *dark* and read them aloud. You can use these words when you talk about color. The flowers are light yellow. Ask children to come up with sentences using colors and the words *light* and *dark.*

If... children have difficulty recognizing words from the word list,

then... use the High-Frequency Word Activities on p. T•9.

On Their Own Assign Worktext p. 44 for practice.

Mini-Lesson 3

Remind children that...
- *describing* is painting a picture with words.
- objects can be described by their numbers and colors.

Word List

eighty	seventy
fifty	sixty
forty	ten
hundred	thirty
ninety	twenty

Guide Practice

Write the number words from the Word List. These are words for numbers. This is the number ten. Say the word with me: *ten.* Point to *ten* and write the numeral 10 next to the word. If you add ten to ten, you get *twenty.* That is the next number on the list. Say the word with me: *twenty.* Point to *twenty* and write the numeral 20 next to the word. All these numbers end in zero. Go through all the numbers in the list, asking children to repeat after you.

We can use these number words to describe or talk about things. Provide an example sentence with the word *twenty*: My brother is twenty years old. Ask children to use words from the Word List in sentences.

If... children have difficulty using number words in sentences,

then... suggest things that might be described using these words, such as ages, measurements, temperatures, and sports scores.

On Their Own Read the directions on Worktext p. 45 to children and assign the page.

Descriptive Words: Size, Shape, and Texture

Objectives:
- Learn words for size, shape, and texture.
- Describe objects using new vocabulary.

MATERIALS
Worktext pp. 46–48

Set the scene Introduce the concept of using words for size, shape, and texture to describe. We use our senses to learn about things. We can then use words to tell about the things we learn. Words such as *huge, square,* and *smooth* help us picture how things look and feel.

Model and teach Model how to describe a scene using words for size, shape, and texture. We have learned how to use words for number and color to talk about what we see. We can also describe things by talking about their shape and size. Words for texture, or how something feels, also help us describe things.

Draw a rectangle. This shape is a rectangle. Many objects I see every day have this shape, such as windows, doors, basketball courts, and picture frames. I can use the word *rectangle* and words for size to talk about these objects. For example: *The picture frame I decorated is a long rectangle.*

If I tell you "Last week I went to a park with my friends," you won't be able to picture my friends and me in the park. Or if you do see a park, it might not look like the park I am talking about. If I say, "Last week I went to a *huge* park. I sat with my friends in a *circle*. We were near some *tall* trees. The grass was very *soft*." The words *huge, circle, tall,* and *soft* all help you picture the park.

Mini-Lesson 1

Remind children that...
- when they describe, they tell about something and paint a picture with words.
- words for shapes and sizes help us talk about what we see.

Word List
big	short
circle	square
heart	star
little	tall
rectangle	triangle

Guide Practice
Draw a *square, rectangle, triangle, circle, star,* and *heart.* Write the words next to the pictures. Ask children to identify each shape and repeat the words multiple times. Point to the triangle.

- What is this shape? (a triangle)
- What makes a triangle different than a circle? (It has straight lines.)
- What makes a triangle different than a square? (It has three sides.)

Draw another triangle that is either much smaller or larger than the original triangle. Ask children to identify the big and small triangle one at a time.

Then draw a basic square house with a triangle roof, rectangle door, and large square windows. Ask children to identify the shapes. Then draw a smaller window in the door and ask children which window is big and which is little.

If... children have difficulty identifying the shapes,
then... erase parts of the picture so only single shapes are showing.

On Their Own Assign Worktext p. 46 to children.

Mini-Lesson 2

Remind children that...
- *describing* is painting a picture with words.
- words for shape, size, and texture help us describe things.

Word List

bumpy	round
large	small
long	smooth
oval	soft
rough	tiny

Guide Practice

Write the words from the Word List. Read through the list and say each word aloud. Ask the class to repeat. Point to the word *smooth*.

- What is this word? (*smooth*)
- What are some things you know that are smooth?

(Possible responses: ice, my desk, the gym floor, my dog's fur)
- What is a word that means *not* smooth? (Possible responses: *rough, bumpy.* Point out any words from the Word List that children mention.)

Continue in this way with several words from the Word List, giving examples and non-examples for each. Then model using the words in a sentence: The long hallway has a smooth floor. Ask children to come up with their own sentences. Encourage them to think of descriptive words that are not on the Word List.

If... children have difficulty using descriptive words, **then...** create sentences that are missing adjectives, such as *The (blank) mouse had (blank) fur.* Ask children to fill in the blanks.

On Their Own Assign Worktext p. 47 to children.

Mini-Lesson 3

Remind children that...
- *describing* is painting a picture with words.
- there are many kinds of descriptive words.

Word List

furry	slow
huge	soft
loud	thick
quick	thin
quiet	wide

Guide Practice

Tell children that to describe, they should use words for shapes, sizes, and textures. When they describe some things, such as animals, it is also helpful to describe how the thing moves or sounds. Ask children to name an animal they have seen. Children may name a pet or a zoo animal. Give the following prompts and questions. Write

the words from the Word List to give children ideas of descriptive words that they can use.

- Describe the animal's skin or fur. Is it thick? Is it furry or soft?
- Describe the animal's size and shape. How tall is it? Does it have a wide body or a long neck? How big is it?
- How does the animal move? What kinds of sounds does the animal make?

If... children have difficulty describing an animal in detail,
then... model a description using words from the Word List.

On Their Own With children, name each animal pictured on Worktext p. 48. Then assign the page.

Descriptive Words: Common Events

Objectives:
- Learn words used to describe common events.
- Describe common events and activities.

MATERIALS
Worktext pp. 49–51

Set the scene
Introduce to children the concept of description. To describe means to tell about, or paint a picture with words. Tell children that they go places and do things every day. Sometimes it's fun to tell about where they were and what they did. The best way to tell about what they did is to give good descriptions.

Model and teach
Model giving a detailed description of a common event. When I say I took a trip to the beach, you have some idea of what I mean. To really explain what it was like, I need to tell more about my trip: what I did, what I saw, and how I felt. I might say something like, "I went to the beach. It was on the ocean. The sand was white and hot. It burned my feet. I had to walk quickly until I got to the wet sand closer to the water. The air smelled salty. The water was cold. The waves were bigger than I am. I saw a starfish. I picked up a lot of shells. I made a sand castle. I had a lot of fun." Now you can imagine my trip. Even if you had never been to a beach, you would have some idea of how a beach looks, smells, and feels. You also know from my description what I did at the beach and how I felt about it.

Mini-Lesson 1

Remind children that...
- *describing* means telling about things we see and do.
- answering questions about *who, what,* and *where* helps us describe.

Word List

do	see
food	what
fun	where
go	who
good	with

Guide Practice
Write *where, what,* and *who.* Read the words aloud. We are going to talk about things we do and places we go. When you talk about things that you do, think of these words and questions. *Where* did you go? *What* did you do? *What* did you see? *Who* were you with?

Ask children to describe a trip to a place many of them have been to. It could be a skating rink, a bowling alley, a local park, or a nearby city. Ask questions such as the following: What did you see? How did you feel? Did you have fun? What sounds and smells do you remember? Read aloud the Word List and encourage children to use words from the list to describe their trip.

If... children have difficulty describing events using details,
then... ask more specific questions such as "What food tasted sweet or salty?" and "How many people were there?"

On Their Own Ask children to complete Worktext p. 49.

Mini-Lesson 2

Remind children that...
- *describing* means telling about things we see and do.
- when we talk about activities, we can use the words *first, then, after,* and *last* to explain what we did.

Word List

after	last
camp	party
first	sad
game	school
happy	then

Guide Practice

Today we will practice telling about activities that we do. Write *party, game, camp,* and *school.* Say the words aloud and have children repeat after you. Then have children help you describe an activity they have participated in. It can be an activity from the Word List or another, such as skating or bicycling. Ask questions like these:

- What did you do?
- Where did you do it? When?
- What did you do first? What did you do after that? What happened last?
- How did you feel about it? Were you happy or sad?

Encourage children to add as many details to their descriptions as possible. Try to prompt children to use the sequence words from the Word List.

If... children have difficulty describing what they do, **then...** ask them more specific questions, such as "What were you wearing? What was it like outside?"

On Their Own Assign Worktext p. 50 for practice.

Mini-Lesson 3

Remind children that...
- *describing* means telling about things we see and do.
- we can use details to describe events like parties and holidays.

Word List

celebration	music
family	parade
flag	park
gather	picnic
meal	treat

Guide Practice

Write *celebration, gather,* and *family.* Ask children to think of other words that have to do with celebrations. Today we will talk about special days when we celebrate something. A *celebration* is when you gather, or come together, with your family or your friends. Celebrations are about having fun.

Write *park, picnic, parade, music,* and *flag.* Say the words, and ask children to repeat after you. Let's begin by talking about the Fourth of July. Last Fourth of July, I went to a park. My family had a picnic. I saw a parade and heard music. I waved a flag. Ask children to tell about their celebrations. Encourage them to include many details. Read aloud the words from the Word List, and encourage children to use some of them in their descriptions.

If... children have difficulty creating detailed descriptions, **then...** ask them to describe another celebration, such as their favorite birthday. Ask specific questions.

On Their Own Have children complete Worktext p. 51. Encourage children to ask each other questions about the celebrations they created from the pictures.

Vocabulary Lesson 8
Time and Order Words

Objectives:
- Learn words for time and order.
- Identify and use words for time and order in sentences.

MATERIALS
Worktext pp. 52–54

Set the scene Introduce to children the need for time and order words. Explain that they use words for time and order every day. Words like *Tuesday, yesterday*, and *last week* show time. Words like *before, after*, and *next* show order. Encourage children to use these words to tell stories or to talk about their day.

Model and teach Model for children how to include words for time in their descriptions. I am going to tell you about what I did this week: *This week I went to school. I stayed home. I went out to dinner. I went to the zoo.* Now I am going to tell you about my week again. This time I will not just tell you *what* I did, but *when* I did those things. Emphasize the days of the week in the following sentences. *This week I went to school on Monday, Tuesday, Wednesday, Thursday, and Friday. On Saturday and Sunday I stayed home and played with friends. Thursday night I went out to dinner. Sunday morning I went to the zoo.* Whenever I talk about something, I should say what happened and when it happened.

Show children how to use words for order. Write *first, next,* and *last.* Read the words aloud with children. Now I will tell you about my morning. Point to the sequence words as appropriate. The *first* thing I did was wake up. *Next,* I brushed my teeth and ate breakfast. *Last,* I got in my car and drove to school. The words *first, next,* and *last* tell you the order of what I did this morning.

Mini-Lesson 1

Remind children that...
- words for time and order help us talk about when things happened.
- we can use words for time and order to talk about our lives.

Word List

first	Saturday
Friday	Sunday
last	Thursday
Monday	Tuesday
next	Wednesday

Guide Practice
Read aloud the Word List. Guide children in using words for sequence and the days of the week in sentences. Use the following model as a guide.

- What day of the week is it?
- What is your favorite day of the week?
- Think about last Saturday. What is the first thing you did? (Possible answer: First, I ate breakfast.)
- What did you do next on Saturday? (Possible answer: Next, I played games.)
- What did you do last on Saturday? (Possible answer: Last, I read a bedtime story with my dad.)

Encourage children to use time or order words in their descriptions.

If... children have difficulty using words for time and order in their descriptions,
then... model describing your favorite day of the week, and then ask children to try again.

On Their Own Have children complete Worktext p. 52.

Mini-Lesson 2

Remind children that...
- words for time and order tell when events happened.
- these words help us tell stories and talk about our lives.

Word List

after	today
before	tomorrow
during	yesterday
later	now
then	when

Guide Practice

Read aloud the Word List to children. Choose two to three words to model correct time order. Before school, I woke up, brushed my teeth, and got in my car. During school, I talk to you about words for time and order. After school, I will go home. Then ask children to provide their own examples.

Then write the words *yesterday, today,* and *tomorrow* from the Word List. Have children take turns sharing what they did yesterday, what they did today, and what they plan to do tomorrow.

If... children have difficulty using words from the Word List in the correct order,

then... display a timeline and put sequence words on the timeline in the correct order, such as *before, now,* and *later.*

On Their Own Assign Worktext p. 53 to children.

Mini-Lesson 3

Remind children that...
- words for time and order help us talk about when things happened.
- we can use words for time and order to talk about our lives.

Word List

August	**July**
begin	June
evening	morning
finally	soon
finish	while

Guide Practice

Write *begin* and *finish.* Everything we do *begins,* or *starts,* and *finishes,* or ends. Summer *begins* in June and *finishes* in August. You know words for time and order, like *first, next,* and *last.* Today we're going to use these words to talk about things we do in the summer. Use the following model as a guide.

- Imagine that it is a Friday morning in June. How do you begin your day? (Possible answer: I begin the day by walking my dog with my mom.)
- Write *while.* The word *while* means "at the same time as." What happens *while* you walk the dog? (Possible response: While we walk the dog, she starts to chase a squirrel.)
- What do you do later in the day? (Possible answer: Later, we make hamburgers.)
- Now, without me asking you questions, tell me about your summer day. Use some of the time and order words we learned.

If... children have difficulty using time and order words to talk about a day,

then... model describing a basic activity, like making a sandwich, using words for time and order.

On Their Own Assign Worktext p. 54 to children.

Vocabulary Lesson 9
Dictionary/Glossary

Objectives:
- Learn the purpose of a dictionary/glossary.
- Learn how to use a dictionary/glossary.

MATERIALS
Worktext pp. 55–57

Set the scene Introduce to children the concept of using a dictionary. Explain that a *dictionary* is a book or list of words and their meanings. Today they will learn how to use a dictionary. They will learn how words are organized in a dictionary.

Model and teach Tell children that a dictionary is a book of words and their meanings. Some dictionaries have pictures. Many dictionaries list information about the word, like how to say it. To make the book easy to use, words in a dictionary are listed in ABC order. So words that start with a come before words that start with b, and so on. The list goes on through the rest of the alphabet. The words within each letter's section are also in *ABC* order.

When I want to find a word in the dictionary, I start by looking at the first letter. Then I go to the section of the dictionary that starts with that letter. Once I am in that section, I look for words that have the same second letter. **Write each word and group of letters (excluding hyphens) so you can point to them as you explain how they are alphabetized.** If I want to look up the word *asleep* in a dictionary, I first look at the *a* part. Then I look for words that begin with *as-*. I know I will find *as-* words after *ar-* words because *r* comes before *s* in the alphabet. I know I will find *as-* words before *at-* words because *s* comes before *t*. So *asleep* will be after *arm* and before *ate* in the dictionary.

Mini-Lesson 1

Remind children that...
- a dictionary is a book of words.
- words in a dictionary are listed in *ABC* order.

Word List
anteater	daily
bell	empty
bib	hill
bicycle	kind
bill	zipper

Guide Practice
Write the words *anteater* and *zipper*. Say the words aloud and have children repeat them. Would the word *anteater* be near the beginning or near the end of a dictionary? (beginning) Does the word *zipper* come before or after the word *anteater*? (after) If possible, look up the words *anteater* and *zipper* in a children's dictionary. Share the definitions or pictures with the class.

Write the words *bib, bicycle,* and *bill.* Say the words aloud and have children repeat. Point out that these words all begin with the letters *bi.* These words appear near each other in a dictionary.

If... children have difficulty understanding how a dictionary is organized,
then... see Lesson 3 for additional practice and explanations of alphabetization.

On Their Own Read the directions at the top of Worktext p. 55 and assign the page.

Mini-Lesson 2

Remind children that...
- a dictionary is a book of words.
- words in a dictionary are listed in *ABC* order.

Word List

afternoon	float
believe	hunter
blizzard	nail
bounce	once
dare	reach

Guide Practice

Write *town.* Above it write *rake, read, rough,* and *rug.* We want to find the entry word *town* in the dictionary. It will be listed in dark print. The four words above it are *guide words.* Explain that guide words tell the first word and last word on the page. Children can use the guide words to help them quickly find the word they're looking for.

- What section of the dictionary will the word *reach* be in? (the *r* section)
- Let's look at the guide words. Will you find *reach* before or after *rug*? How do you know? (Possible response: before because *e* comes before *u* in *ABC* order)

Continue in this way until children see that *reach* comes between *rake* and *read.* Then show the word *reach* in a dictionary and read its definition.

If... children have difficulty using guide words,
then... ask children to volunteer words to look up and provide additional practice using an actual children's dictionary.

On Their Own Have children work through Worktext p. 56.

Mini-Lesson 3

Remind children that...
- a dictionary is a book of words.
- a dictionary provides definitions, example sentences, and parts of speech.

Word List

blossom	holiday
elk	passenger
catch	sail
expect	surprise
few	under

Guide Practice

Some dictionaries include sentences or phrases that show you how to use the word. Use the following model to instruct children. Select an entry that includes a sample sentence.

- Let's look up the word *elk.* What is the definition of the word? (Possible response: a deer with long antlers)
- How is it used in a phrase or sentence in the dictionary? (Possible response: The elk grazed in the field.)
- Now let's use it in a sentence of our own: *Have you ever seen an elk or a moose?* Give children the opportunity to say their own sentences.

Explain to children that a dictionary can give the pronunciation, or how the word sounds. Explain that a part of speech tells whether the word is an action word, an object word, or some other kind of word.

If... children have difficulty recognizing the different parts of a dictionary entry,
then... show multiple examples from an actual children's dictionary.

On Their Own Have children work through Worktext p. 57.

Sort Words: Two Categories

Objectives:

- Understand positive and negative groupings (that one group can be made from alike things and another group can be made of things that are not like the first group).
- Sort words into two categories.

MATERIALS

Worktext pp. 58–60

Set the scene Introduce to children the concept of sorting words. Putting words into groups helps us learn words. Today we are going to look at words that can go together.

Model and teach Model for children sorting words for objects into groups. I have some things here. I want to see what groups I can make with them. Show children a pen, a crayon, and a marker. Other writing utensils may also be used. First, I need to look at each object and name it. I see a *pen* and a *crayon*. Point to each object as you name it. Then, I will think about each word. I know a pen and a crayon are things I write or draw with. I also see a marker. I can say these are all things I write or draw with. They are alike. We can sort things that are alike together.

Let's make another group. We will call the group "things we cannot write or draw with." What are some words that go in this group? Ask children to point out classroom objects that are not writing utensils, such as a map, a desk, and a stapler. I know that I cannot write or draw with a map, a desk, or a stapler. These words can go in the group "things we cannot write or draw with."

Remind children that...

- sorting words into groups helps us learn words.
- words can be put into groups of things that go together and things that do not go with that group.

Word List

bed	group
body	hand
ear	hat
flower	puzzle
foot	train

Guide Practice

Display pictures on Worktext p. 58. Have children help you make two groups with these pictures.

- Can you put the *hand* and *foot* pictures in a group? (yes) How? (Possible response: *Hand* and *foot* are parts of the body.)

- Which other pictures are parts of the body? (ear and nose)
- What can we call this group of pictures? (Possible response: parts of the body)
- What pictures are left? (flower, bed, hat, and puzzle)
- Do the other pictures belong together? (no)
- What can we call these pictures to show that they are not body parts? (things that are not parts of the body)

If... children have difficulty understanding the basis of forming positive and negative groups,

then... ask children to name things and consider whether or not they belong in the main group (parts of the body).

On Their Own Assign Worktext p. 58 for practice.

Mini-Lesson 2

Remind children that...
- sorting words into groups helps us learn words.
- words can be put into groups of things that go together and things that do not go with that group.

Word List

chair	nine
eight	number
five	pencil
group	sign
horse	two

Guide Practice

Show the pictures on Worktext p. 59. Name them and have children repeat: *eight, five, pencil, sign, horse, nine, chair,* and *two.* Point to the eight.

- What is this a picture of? (eight) What is eight? (a number)

- Is there another picture of a number? (yes) What is it? (Possible responses: two, five, nine)
- We can put these words in a group called *numbers.* Write *Numbers.* Below it, write the word *eight* and any other numbers children have identified.
- Let's see if any other pictures belong in this group. Children should identify the remaining numbers. Add these numbers to the list.
- Now let's look at the pictures that are left. Do any of them name numbers? (no) That's right. We can make two groups—*numbers* and *not numbers.*

If... children have difficulty understanding how some things go together as a positive group and others go together as a negative group,

then... point to each pictures and ask, "Is this a number or not?"

On Their Own Have children work through Worktext p. 59.

Mini-Lesson 3

Remind children that...
- sorting words into groups helps us learn words.
- words can be put into groups of things that go together and things that do not go with that group.

Word List

robin	garden
eagle	cracker
rooster	alike
parrot	unalike
ladder	fifteen

Guide Practice

Write *robin, ladder, rooster, fifteen, cracker, garden, eagle,* and *parrot.* Say each word, and ask children to repeat after you. After discussing each word, help children see that some of the words belong together, or are *alike.* Write *alike.*

- Point to the word *robin.* What is this word? (robin)
- What is a robin? (Possible response: a small bird)
- What is another word for a kind of bird? (Possible response: eagle)

These words are *alike* because they name kinds of birds. Continue in this way until all the birds are grouped together. Then explain to children that the rest of the words may be put in a group called *not birds.*

If... children have difficulty understanding how some things go together as a positive group and others go together as a negative group,

then... concentrate on the positive group first. Then ask such questions as, "Is a ladder a type of bird?"

On Their Own Have children work through Worktext p. 60.

Sort Words: Multiple Categories

Objectives:
- Sort words into multiple categories.
- Recognize similarities between words in word groups.

MATERIALS

Worktext pp. 61–63

Set the scene Explain to children that putting words into groups helps us see how the words are alike. Tell them that today they will look at pictures or words and then put the pictures or words into groups.

Model and teach Tell children that you will sort several pictures into groups. Draw or show pictures of a square and a triangle, a hammer and a nail, and a flower and a tree. First, I need to look at each picture and name it. Name each picture and ask children to repeat after you. Then I will think about each word. I will think about how the words are alike. Point to the *flower* image. This picture shows a flower. The word *flower* names something that grows in the ground. I will look at the other pictures to see if there is another thing that grows in the ground. I see a tree. The words *tree* and *flower* are alike. They both name things that grow in the ground. Circle the *flower* and *tree* pictures, or indicate in some other way that they are grouped together.

Have children help you group the remaining pictures. After they have identified the groups *shapes* (square and triangle) and *things you build with* (hammer and nail), review the groups with children. Make sure they understand why the pictures are arranged in these groups.

Mini-Lesson 1

Remind children that...
- sorting words into groups helps us learn words.
- words that name similar things can be put into a group.

Word List

four	ear
three	hat
two	coat
six	pants
knee	shoes

Guide Practice

Display the pictures on Worktext p. 61. Name and briefly discuss each picture. Then have children help you make three groups with these pictures. Begin by asking children to talk about one of the pictures.

- What is this? Yes, it is a number. It is the number three.
- Is three the only number? (no) What other numbers do you see? (Possible responses: two, four, six)
- These words are alike because they name numbers. They can go in a group called *numbers*. What other pictures go in this group?

Guide children in grouping the rest of the pictures. When all the pictures are grouped, have children name the pictures in each group and tell why the pictures are grouped together.

If... children have difficulty understanding how to form groups,

then... ask them more questions about the members of the groups so they can see what each group member has in common.

On Their Own Assign Worktext p. 61 to children.

Mini-Lesson 2

Remind children that...
- sorting words into groups helps us learn words.
- words can be put into groups of things that are alike.

Word List

apple	man
baby	pizza
banana	train
child	truck
hamburger	woman

Guide Practice

Show the pictures on Worktext p. 62. Name each picture and have children repeat after you. Point to the picture of pizza.

- What does this picture show? (pizza) What is pizza? (Possible response: food)

- What other picture of food do you see? (Possible response: hamburger) We can put these words in a group called *food*.
- Now point to the picture of the train. What does this picture show? (train) Since a train is not a food, the word *train* goes in a different group.
- What is a train? (Possible responses: something that moves, something you ride in)

Continue in this way until children identify all three groups: *foods, people,* and *things you ride in.*

If... children have difficulty sorting,

then... point to two pictures that go together, and ask how the pictures are alike. Once children can recognize the similarity, ask them to find another picture that is like those two.

On Their Own Have children work through Worktext p. 62.

Mini-Lesson 3

Remind children that...
- sorting words into groups helps us learn words.
- words can be put into groups of things that are alike.

Word List

aunt	ketchup
uncle	television
April	radio
May	basement
mustard	kitchen

Guide Practice

Write *mustard, aunt, April, uncle, ketchup,* and *May.* Ask children to read the words along with you.

- Point to the word *ketchup.* What is this word? (*ketchup*)
- What is ketchup? (Possible response: something you put on food to give it a tomato taste)

- What is another word for something you put on your food? (mustard)

These words are alike because they both name things you put on food. What other words belong in this group?

Continue in this way until all three pairings are made. Then ask children to give an additional word that belongs in each group.

If... children have difficulty understanding how to group the words,

then... tell them the group names, and go through the list of words asking such questions as, "Is a kitchen a member of a family?"

On Their Own With children, read through each word on Worktext p. 63. Then assign the page.

Vocabulary Lesson 12
Unfamiliar Words

Objectives:
- Learn to use context clues to identify meanings of unfamiliar words.
- Recognize definitions, synonyms and antonyms, and examples as context clues.

MATERIALS

Worktext pp. 64–66

Set the scene Tell children that as they read they will often see a word they don't know. One way to find the meaning of an unfamiliar word is to look in a dictionary or glossary. Another way is to read the words and sentences around the word and look for clues.

Model and teach Write *He was starting to annoy, or bother, me a lot.* Read the sentence aloud with children. Underline *annoy.* If I read this sentence and do not know the word *annoy,* I look at the rest of the sentence for clues. This sentence tells me that the word *annoy* means "bother." Underline *bother.* Circle *or.* The word *or* introduces the meaning. I could also look up the word in a dictionary.

Teach children to also look for examples in sentences that contain unfamiliar words. Write *The cake recipe has many ingredients, such as sugar and eggs.* Underline *ingredients.* I want to figure out the meaning of the word *ingredients.* Point to *such as sugar and eggs.* Explain that the words *such as* introduce examples. *Sugar* and *eggs* are examples of what *ingredients* means. I know that you use eggs and sugar when you bake a cake. Ingredients must mean "things you use to cook something."

Explain to children that another strategy for finding the meaning of an unfamiliar word is to look up the word in a dictionary. If a dictionary is not available to them, they can also use the context of a sentence to figure out the meaning. Refer to Lessons 18 and 19.

Mini-Lesson 1

Remind children that...
- clue words in sentences can help us learn unfamiliar words.
- some sentences include words that define or tell more about an unfamiliar word.

Word List

chick	lovely
crib	navy
ewe	raft
foal	stare
gate	trout

Guide Practice

Write *The foal, a baby horse named Joe, likes to eat hay.* Read the sentence aloud. Point to *foal.* This is the word *foal.* Let's look at the sentence for clues to what *foal* means.

- Point to the commas in the sentence. What words are in between the commas? (a baby horse) Circle *a baby horse.*
- What do these words tell about? (foal) Underline *foal.*
- What do you think a *foal* is? (a baby horse) That's right. A *foal* is a baby horse. In this sentence, the baby horse is named Joe.

Continue in the same way with this sentence: *Grandma's hat is lovely, or very pretty.* Point out that the word *or* signals that a meaning follows.

If... children have difficulty understanding how the phrases can help them,

then... read the sentences without those words. Then read the complete sentence again and discuss the clues that the words give to the reader.

On Their Own Have children work through Worktext p. 64.

Mini-Lesson 2

Remind children that...
- examples within a sentence help us figure out the meanings of unfamiliar words.
- examples are often introduced by such words as *like*, *such as*, and *for example*.

Word List

attractions	performers
creatures	stunts
for example	such as
gear	supplies
like	warnings

Guide Practice

Focus on identifying examples that explain unfamiliar words in sentences. Write *We saw all kinds of performers, like singers, dancers, and jugglers.* Read the sentence aloud with children.

- Let's figure out what *performers* means by looking at the rest of the sentence.
- What clue word do you see? (*like*)
- Which words come after the word *like*? (*singers, dancers, and jugglers*)
- The word *performers* is right before the clue word *like*, so singers, dancers, and jugglers are examples of performers. How could you define *performers*? (Possible response: people who act in a show)

Explain that *such as* and *for example* also introduce examples.

If... children have difficulty identifying clue words that could be used instead of *like*,

then... model saying the sentence with the new clue word. Ask children if the sentence makes sense. Then have them join you in saying the new sentence.

On Their Own Assign Worktext p. 65 for practice.

Mini-Lesson 3

Remind children that...
- clues in a sentence often help us figure out the meanings of unfamiliar words.
- synonyms and antonyms are kinds of clues.

Word List

adores	gigantic
but	remembered
chuckled	revealed
dull	too
exhausted	wild

Guide Practice

Tell children that synonyms and antonyms can work as clues. *Synonyms* are words that mean nearly the same thing. *Antonyms* are words for opposites. Guide children using synonyms and antonyms to explain unfamiliar words. Write *My dad adores that dog, and my mom loves it too.*

- What does *loves* mean? (Possible response: really likes)
- The clue word *too* tells us that *adores* and *loves* are the same. So what does *adores* mean? (Possible answer: really likes)
- Are *adores* and *loves* synonyms? (yes)

Write and read aloud: *That book is interesting, but this one is dull.* The clue word *but* tells us that *interesting* and *dull* are different.

Follow the same procedure with other words from the Word Lists.

If... children have difficulty identifying words as synonyms or antonyms,

then... ask them if the sentences are saying the two things are alike or different. Remind them of the clue words *too* for synonyms and *but* for antonyms.

On Their Own Assign Worktext p. 66 for practice.

Suffix -*ly*

Objectives:

- Learn to identify base words and suffixes.
- Learn the meanings of words ending in -*ly* and their base words.

MATERIALS

Worktext pp. 67–69

Set the scene Emphasize to children that looking at word structure, or the different parts of a word, can help them figure out the meaning of unfamiliar words. Introduce the concept of suffixes to children. Explain that a *suffix* is a word part that is added to the end of a word. Adding a suffix to a word changes the word's meaning. Today they will learn about the suffix -*ly*.

Model and teach Write *safely*. The word *safely* ends with the suffix -*ly*. The suffix -*ly* means "in a certain way." *Safely* means "in a safe way." Model how to find the base word of a word with a suffix. Here is how I read a word with a suffix. First, I look at the base word. A *base word* is a word without any added word parts. Cover *ly* and read the base word *safe*. The word *safe* is the base word of the word *safely*. After I read the base word, I read the base word and the suffix together. Run your hand under the word parts as you read: *safe, ly, safely*. An example sentence is *We got home safely*.

Follow the same procedure with the word *clearly*. *Clearly* means "in a clear way." An example sentence is *The boy sang the song very clearly*.

The suffix -*ly* usually means "in a certain way," but when the base word shows time, it can also mean "how often." Think of the word *weekly*. The base word of *weekly* is *week*. Instead of saying "We have choir practice every week," you can say "We have choir practice weekly." The word *weekly* means "every week."

Emphasize to children that looking at word structure, or the different parts of a word, can help them figure out the meaning of unfamiliar words.

Mini-Lesson 1

Remind children that...

- some words have a word part at the end.
- the suffix -*ly* means "in a certain way."

Word List

loud	nicely
loudly	quiet
neat	quietly
neatly	sad
nice	sadly

Guide Practice

Focus on the word *quiet*. When I say *Please be quiet*, you know that means to please not talk or make much noise.

- If I add the letters *l* and *y* to the word *quiet*, I make a new word. Write *ly*.
- Say the word *quiet*, point to the *l* and the y, and say -*ly. Quiet, ly, Quietly.* Let's all say it together. *Quiet, ly,*

Quietly. Quietly means "in a quiet way." If I say "Please talk quietly," how do I want you to talk? (Children may speak softly to give you an example.)

Follow the same procedure with the words *loud, neat, sad,* and *nice*.

If... children have difficulty understanding the suffix -*ly*, **then...** provide additional example sentences for the -*ly* words in the Word List.

On Their Own Assign Worktext p. 67 to children.

Mini-Lesson 2

Remind children that...
- a suffix comes at the end of the word and changes the meaning of the word.
- the suffix *-ly* means "in a certain way" or "how often."

Word List

fair	hourly
fairly	kind
glad	kindly
gladly	wild
hour	wildly

Guide Practice
Write the words *gladly*, *fairly*, and *wildly*. Have children read the words with you. Point to the word *gladly*.

- What is this word? (gladly)
- What is the base word of the word *gladly*? (glad)

- What does the word *glad* mean? (Possible responses: happy, cheerful)
- Since the base word is *glad,* what does *gladly* mean? (Possible responses: in a cheerful way, in a glad way)
- Tell me a sentence that includes the word *gladly.* (Possible responses: She gladly finished her homework; I'd gladly take care of your dog while you're on vacation.)

Follow the same procedure for the words *fairly* and *wildly.* Then write the word *hourly.* Explain that, because the word *hour* shows time, *hourly* means "every hour."

If... children cannot supply a definition in words, **then...** have them act it out, if possible. For example, prompt them by asking, "How does someone wave *gladly*?"

On Their Own With children, name the *-ly* words found on Worktext p. 68 and assign the page.

Mini-Lesson 3

Remind children that...
- a suffix comes at the end of the word and changes the meaning of the word.
- the suffix *-ly* means "in a certain way" or "how often."

Word List

brave	monthly
bravely	sudden
light	suddenly
lightly	sweet
month	sweetly

Guide Practice
Write *bravely*, *lightly*, *suddenly*, and *sweetly*. Point to the word *lightly*.

- What is this word? (lightly)
- What is the base word of the word *lightly?* (light)

- What does the word *light* mean? (Possible responses: not heavy, bright) If children only think of *light* as in sunlight or daylight, explain that the word *light* has multiple meanings. Tell them that *light* in the word *lightly* means "not heavy" or "gentle." Model for children touching or tapping something lightly.
- What does *lightly* mean? (in a light way, in a gentle way)
- Tell me a sentence with *lightly.* (Possible responses: My mother lightly touched my shoulder when it was time to leave.)

Follow the same procedure for rest of the words. Tell children that *sweet* can mean "sugary" or "pleasant."

If... children cannot use a word in a sentence, **then...** prompt with questions, such as "When did someone you know act bravely?"

On Their Own Assign Worktext p. 69 for practice.

Vocabulary Lesson 14
Multiple-Meaning Words

Objectives:
- Understand the concept of multiple-meaning words.
- Identify multiple-meaning words and use them in sentences.

MATERIALS
Worktext pp. 70–72

Set the scene Explain that multiple-meaning words are words that have more than one meaning. They mean different things at different times. Provide the word *wave* as an example. Tell children it can mean moving your hand back and forth to say hello. It can also mean the way the water moves at the beach. Tell children that today they will look at words that have more than one meaning.

Model and teach Write *fair*. Underneath it in a column write: *festival, not stormy, honest, blond*. Read the definitions. The word *fair* can have all these meanings. Point to each meaning as you mention it. The word *fair* can mean "festival." A *street fair* is a festival in the street. *Fair* can also mean "not stormy." *Fair weather* means there are no storms. A *fair deal* means an honest deal. Someone who is *fair-haired* has blond hair.

Ask children to listen to a sentence to see if they can find the right meaning for *fair* in it: *You have to be fair, and let everyone take a turn.*

Go through each meaning of the word *fair*. Show children that the meanings "festival," "not stormy," and "blond" do not make sense in this sentence. Explain that "honest" does make sense because an honest person would let others take turns.

Encourage children to use a dictionary to find the different meanings of a multiple-meaning word. Children should try each meaning in the sentence and choose the one that makes the most sense in the context of the sentence. Refer to Lessons 18 and 19.

Mini-Lesson 1

Remind children that...
- multiple-meaning words look like they are the same word.
- multiple-meaning words mean different things at different times.

Word List
bat	horn
bug	pet
can	ruler
cold	tie
fall	wave

Guide Practice
Use the Word List to introduce additional multiple-meaning words. Start with the word *bug*. Hold up a picture of a bug. This is a bug. Say the word with me: *bug*.

- A sentence using the word *bug* is *The bug was just an inch long.* What is this kind of bug? (Possible response: an insect)
- I know another meaning for *bug*. A sentence using the word *bug* is *I caught a flu bug.*
- What is this meaning of *bug*? (Possible response: "a germ")

Follow the same procedure with other words from the Word List.

If... children have trouble understanding a meaning, **then...** model examples of it with other sentences, gestures, or drawings.

On Their Own Have children complete Worktext p. 70.

Mini-Lesson 2

Remind children that...
- multiple-meaning words look like they are the same word.
- substituting each meaning into a sentence can help them figure out the correct meaning.

Word List

bear	duck
bed	fan
block	key
bulb	rock
cap	shade

Guide Practice

Use the words in the Word List to introduce additional multiple-meaning words. Write the sentence *The duck ate from my hand.* Read the sentence aloud and point to the word *duck.*

- Say the word with me: *duck.* I know that *duck* can have more than one meaning. Let's think of different meanings for *duck.* (Possible responses: "an animal with feathers that lives in ponds," "to bend down to get away from something")
- Now let's see which definition works in our sentence. Try each definition in the sentence.
- Which definition makes sense? ("an animal with feathers that lives in ponds")

Continue in this way using the following sentences: *The* bear *went up the tree. I stood by the* fan *to get cool.* Rock *the baby gently. She pressed the piano* key.

If... children can't decide which is the correct definition,
then... encourage them to act out the sentences.

On Their Own Assign Worktext p. 71 for practice.

Mini-Lesson 3

Remind children that...
- multiple-meaning words mean different things at different times.
- clue words in sentences can help them figure out the correct meaning to use.

Word List

bank	right
bark	second
lap	taste
present	train
rest	watch

Guide Practice

Write *The dog likes to bark at the mailman.* Underline the word *bark.* Read the sentence with children.

- What are some meanings of the word *bark*? ("part of a tree," "make a loud sound")

- What does the sentence tell you about the word *bark*? (The dog likes to do it at the mailman.)
- What words in the sentence help you know what *bark* means? (Possible responses: dog, mailman. Circle clue words that children identify.)
- Which meaning of the word *bark* makes sense in this sentence? ("make a loud sound")

Follow the same procedure for other multiple-meaning words from the Word List.

If... children have difficulty looking at an entire sentence for clues,
then... model pointing out clue words and phrases.

On Their Own Have children work through Worktext p. 72.

Vocabulary Lesson 15
Prefixes

Objectives:
- Understand that a prefix comes before a word and changes the meaning of a word.
- Learn how to read and understand words that contain prefixes.

MATERIALS
Worktext pp. 73–75

Set the scene Emphasize to children that looking at word structure, or the different parts of a word, can help them figure out the meaning of unfamiliar words. Introduce the concept of prefixes to children. Explain that some words have a word part called a *prefix* at the beginning. Adding a prefix to a word changes the word's meaning. Different prefixes have different meanings. Knowing prefixes can help children learn new words.

Model and teach Model how to read a word with a prefix. Write *unpack*. *Unpack* begins with the prefix *un-*. The prefix *un-* means "not" or "do the opposite of." This is how I read a word with a prefix. First, I figure out the base word. A *base word* is a word without any added word parts. Cover *un* and read the base word *pack*. The base word of *unpack* is *pack*. I know what *pack* means. It means to put things inside something else. I pack a suitcase when I go on vacation. After I read the base word, I read the prefix. The prefix of *unpack* is *un*. Then, I read the two parts together. Run your hand under the word parts as you read: *un, pack, unpack*. *Unpack* means to do the opposite of *pack*. Since *pack* means "to put in," *unpack* means "to take out." A sentence with *unpack* is *I unpack my suitcase when I get home from vacation.*

Follow the same procedure with the word *unsafe*. *Unsafe* means "not safe." An example sentence is *It's unsafe to cross a street without looking.*

Mini-Lesson 1

Remind children that...
- a prefix is a word part that comes before a word.
- the prefix *un-* means "not" or the "opposite of."

Word List
do	retie
paint	tie
pin	undo
redo	unpin
repaint	untie

Guide Practice
Use the Word List to continue teaching about prefixes. Write *re-*. When the prefix *re-* comes before a word, it means "again." Let's think about the word *repaint*. Say the word with me: *re-, paint, repaint*. The word *repaint* has the word *paint* in it.

- When I say *I am going to paint a picture*, what does the word *paint* mean? (Possible responses: draw something with color, use paint brushes)
- We know that *re-* means "again." What do you think *repaint* means? (paint again)
- What is a sentence with the word *repaint*? (Possible response: My neighbor is going to repaint his house blue.)

Follow the same procedure with other words from the Word List. These remaining words may be written for children to see and read along with you.

If... children cannot use the word in a sentence, **then...** model a sentence using the word and then have children try again.

On Their Own Help children complete Worktext p. 73.

Mini-Lesson 2

Remind children that...

- a prefix comes before a word and changes the meaning of the word.
- different prefixes have different meanings.

Word List

disagree	mislabel
disappear	misspell
dishonest	mismatch
dislike	mistreat
disobey	misuse

Guide Practice

Use the words in the Word List to teach the prefixes *dis-* and *mis-*. Write *disappear*. *Disappear* begins with the prefix *dis-*. The prefix *dis-* means "the opposite of." When something *appears*, you can see it. Since *disappear* means the opposite of *appear,* when something *disappears* you cannot see it. What is a sentence with the word *disappear*? (Possible response: The magician made the rabbit disappear.)

Write other words from the Word List with the prefix *dis-*. Have children read the words with you. Then identify the prefix and the base word. Have children tell the meaning of the word and use it in a sentence. Explain to children that the prefix *mis-* means "wrong" or "bad." Then follow the same procedure with the remaining words from the Word List.

If... children have difficulty determining the meaning of the base words,

then... give them sample sentences with context clues to help them define the words. Then add the prefix to the words.

On Their Own Assign Worktext p. 74 to children.

Mini-Lesson 3

Remind children that...

- a prefix comes before a word and changes the meaning of the word.
- different prefixes have different meanings.

Word List

impatient	incomplete
imperfect	indefinite
impolite	informal
impossible	incorrect
immature	invisible

Guide Practice

Write *impossible* and *invisible*. Have children read the words with you. With children, identify the base word and the prefix. Explain that the prefixes *in-* and *im-* both mean "not."

- This is the word *invisible*. Cover *visible* with your hand. What is its prefix? (in) That's right. The prefix *in-* means "not."
- Cover *in-* with your hand. The base word is *visible*. What does *visible* mean? (Possible responses: in sight, able to be seen)
- What do you think *invisible* means? (not visible)
- What is a sentence with this word? (Possible response: The spaceship put up a shield that made it in invisible.)

Follow the same procedure with *impossible* and any other words from the Word List. Help children read and understand the meaning of the base words first before discussing the meanings of the whole words.

If... children cannot use the word in a sentence,
then... first model a question using the base word.

On Their Own On Worktext p. 75, read the directions and base words aloud with children. Direct children to complete the page.

Vocabulary Lesson 16
Antonyms

MATERIALS

Worktext pp. 76–78

Set the scene Introduce the concept of antonyms to children. Explain that some words can mean the opposite of other words. *In* is the opposite of *out*. *Up* is the opposite of *down*. *Fast* is the opposite of *slow*. Tell children that words for opposites are called *antonyms*. Today they are going to learn even more antonyms.

Model and teach Write *begin, yes, end, left, no,* and *right*. Point to the words. All these words have an opposite in the list. I am going to match them. Point to *begin*. The first word is *begin*. I know that *begin* means "start." I also know that the opposite of *begin* is *end*. Point to *end*. *End* means "finish." Many things begin and end, like a class, a meal, a story, or a visit. Many places begin and end, too, like a room, a hall, or a street. Write *begin* and *end* next to each other and then point to them as you say the following sentence. *We begin school in September and end in June.*

Follow the same procedure to match *no* to *yes* and *right* to *left*. Discuss the meaning of the first word, saying its antonym. Discuss the meaning of the antonym, and write the words next to each other. Then suggest a sentence or a pair of sentences. Possible sentences: If you brought lunch today, say "yes." If you did not bring lunch, say "no." There is a board to your left and a window to your right. Tell children that if they're not sure whether two words are antonyms, they can look up their definitions in a dictionary.

Mini-Lesson 1

Remind children that...
- some words mean the opposite of other words.
- knowing words for opposites helps us learn words.

Word List

hot	hard
cold	sweet
dry	sour
wet	heavy
soft	light

Guide Practice

Use the Word List to continue teaching antonyms. Write *in* and *out*. Point to the words. These are antonyms that I hear and use all the time, *in* and *out*. Today I want to show the meanings of these words. Stand next to the classroom door.

- Am I in the classroom, or am I out of it? (in)
  Step outside the classroom.
- Now am I in the classroom or out of it? (out)

Follow the same procedure with the other antonym pairs from the Word List. If the words cannot be acted out, provide children with example sentences for each word.

If... children do not understand how the words are opposites,

then... make a drawing or act out the word in an exaggerated way, such as making a face for tasting something sour.

On Their Own Read aloud the directions and all the vocabulary on Worktext p. 76. Ask children to complete the page.

Mini-Lesson 2

Remind children that...
- *antonyms* are words that are opposites.
- we can put words for opposites in pairs.

Word List

big	narrow
empty	small
full	thick
high	thin
low	wide

Guide Practice

Write *empty* and *full.* Let's think about the words *empty* and *full.* They describe opposites.

- What does it mean when something is *empty*? (There is nothing in it.)
- What are some things that can be empty? (Possible responses: a cup, a box, a suitcase)

- Draw a cup. *Full* is the opposite of *empty.* How can a cup that is empty become full? (Possible response: Fill it with water or juice.)
- Color in the cup so it looks full. Is this cup empty or full? (full)
- Now I am going to drink the juice. Erase the color inside the cup. Is the cup full or empty now? (empty)

Follow the same procedure with the other antonym pairs from the list. Use different questions, examples, or drawings to teach children that the words are opposites.

If... children have difficulty understanding the relationship between the antonyms,
then... discuss the meaning of each word and give examples that are familiar to children. For example, a pencil draws a *thin* line, and a marker draws a *thick* line.

On Their Own Assign Worktext p. 77 for practice.

Mini-Lesson 3

Remind children that...
- words for opposites are called *antonyms.*
- many kinds of words, such as words for actions and words to describe, have antonyms.

Word List

always	never
asleep	old
awake	sick
down	up
healthy	young

Guide Practice

Write the antonym pairs and point to them. Today I will play a game with these antonyms. The game is called "It's just the opposite!" I will read a sentence with one of the words on the list. If the sentence is true, nod your head. If the sentence is false, say "It's just the opposite!"

and tell me which word from the list will make it true. Write the following sentences:

- *The sun never rises in the morning.*
- *I close my eyes when I'm asleep.*
- *The rain came up hard.*
- *A healthy person may have a fever.*

Play the game with children. After children have selected a replacement word, have them say the correct sentence aloud.

If... children have difficulty understanding the sentences,
then... discuss the meanings of the antonyms.

On Their Own Direct children to complete Worktext p. 78. After children have matched the cards, ask them to use each word pair in a sentence or pair of sentences.

- ...that
...yms are words that
...ave the same or nearly
the same meaning.
- Identify synonyms and
use them in sentences.

MATERIALS
Worktext pp. 79–81

Set the scene Introduce the concept of synonyms to students. Today we will learn about words that mean the same or almost the same thing. These words are called *synonyms.*

Model and teach Give children examples of synonyms. Explain how the words are alike. When I talk about something, sometimes I can choose between different words. I am going to write a word and think of another word that means the same or almost the same thing. Write *unhappy.* I know that unhappy means "not happy." Another word that means the same thing is *sad.* I can say someone is feeling sad or unhappy and mean the same thing. The words *sad* and *unhappy* are synonyms. Write *sad* next to *unhappy.*

Then teach children that a word can have more than one synonym. Write *big.* I know that *big* means "having a great size," like this. Hold your arms far apart. Another word that means *big* is *large.* Write *large.* There are even more words that mean "having a great size." Write *huge.* Huge means "really big." *Big, large,* and *huge* are all synonyms.

Show how replacing one synonym with another in a sentence does not change the sentence's meaning. Write He had a <u>huge</u> umbrella. Write *big* and *large* above *huge.* If I replace the word *huge* with the word *big* or *large,* the meaning of the sentence does not change. Say the sentences, replacing *huge* with one of the synonyms. Then write *square* and *red* below *huge.* The words *square* and *red* are not synonyms of *huge.* If I put one of these words in the sentence, the meaning changes. Tell children that if they're not sure whether two words are synonyms, they can look up their definitions in a dictionary.

Remind children that...
- some words have the same or nearly the same meaning.
- you can use different words to talk about the same thing.

Word List

boat	ship
drawing	picture
grass	lawn
pants	slacks
rip	tear

Guide Practice
Guide children to help you think of synonyms for various words. Write *boat.* Say the word and have children repeat after you. If possible, show or draw a picture of a boat.

- What do you know about boats? (Possible responses: They float on water. People use them to go places.

They have sails.)
- What is a word that means "big boat"? (Possible response: ship) Write *ship.*
- Do *boat* and *ship* have the same meaning? (no) Do they have almost the same meaning? (yes)
- How are their meanings almost the same? (Possible responses: They both float on water. They both take people places.)

Follow the same procedure with synonym pairs from the Word List: *chair/seat, drawing/picture, little/small, tear/rip,* or *grass/lawn.* Pictures of these words may be found on Worktext p. 79.

If... children have difficulty understanding synonyms, **then...** ask them more questions about the words and draw attention to similarities in meaning.

On Their Own Read aloud the directions on Worktext p. 79 and assign the page.

Mini-Lesson 2

Remind children that...
- *synonyms* are words that have the same or nearly the same meaning.
- synonyms can replace one another in sentences.

Word List

also	nap
chicken	plate
city	rest
dish	too
hen	town

Guide Practice

Work with children to find synonyms for words in sentences. Write *strong*. Say this word with me: *strong*.

- Raise your hand when you see me do something that shows that I am strong. Pantomime walking, lifting weights, and playing a guitar. (Children should raise their hand at lifting weights.) Yes, you need to be strong

to lift something heavy, like weights.
- Write the sentence *The pitcher threw the ball with his powerful arm*. One word in this sentence is a synonym for *strong*.
- Do I need to be a pitcher to lift something heavy? (no)
- Do I need to be a ball to lift something heavy? (no)
- Do I need to be powerful to lift something heavy? (yes)
- *Strong* and *powerful* are synonyms. Circle *strong* and *powerful*. Instead of using the word *powerful*, I could say *The pitcher threw the ball with his strong arm*.

Follow the same procedure with the other synonym pairs from the Word Lists.

If... children have difficulty choosing the synonyms, **then...** make sure they understand each word in the example sentences.

On Their Own Assign Worktext p. 80 for practice.

Mini-Lesson 3

Remind children that...
- words that have the same or nearly the same meaning are called *synonyms*.
- if you replace a word with another word that is not a synonym, the sentence will not have the same meaning.

Word List

begin	ocean
dirty	paste
glue	sea
muddy	sound
noise	start

Guide Practice

Write *My dog enjoys long walks*. Then write *hides* and *likes* above *enjoys*. Read the sentence aloud.

- What does it mean to *enjoy*? (Possible response: to get happiness from)
- Point to *hides*. What does *hides* mean? (Possible

response: puts where no one can see)
- Raise your hand if this sentence makes sense: *My dog hides long walks*. (Children should not raise their hands.) This sentence does not make sense. A long walk is not a thing you can hide. Cross out *hides*.
- What does *likes* mean? (Possible response: enjoys)
- Raise your hand if this sentence means the same thing as the first sentence: *My dog likes long walks*. (Children should raise their hands.) This sentence makes sense. Circle *enjoys* and *likes*. *Enjoys* and *likes* are synonyms.

Follow the same procedure with *start/begin, dirty/muddy, glue/paste, ocean/sea,* or *noise/sound*.

If... children have difficulty replacing the synonyms, **then...** remind them to ask themselves which word makes sense and has the same meaning as the original sentence.

On Their Own Assign Worktext p. 81 for practice.

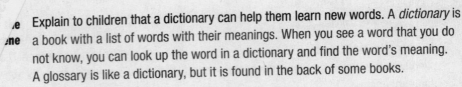

...sary

Explain to children that a dictionary can help them learn new words. A *dictionary* is a book with a list of words with their meanings. When you see a word that you do not know, you can look up the word in a dictionary and find the word's meaning. A glossary is like a dictionary, but it is found in the back of some books.

Model and teach Show a page from a children's dictionary. A dictionary lists words in *ABC* order. Review entry words and guide words with children. Then use the following model to instruct children.

Write *John made a clay plate in art class.* Read the sentence with children, and point to the word *clay*. If I don't know the meaning of the word *clay*, I can find the meaning in the dictionary. First, I use the guide words to find the page that has the word *clay*. Model using guide words and scanning the page to search for the word *clay*. Then I read the definition: "a stiff, sticky kind of earth. Clay can be easily shaped when wet and hardens when it is dried or baked. Bricks, dishes, and vases may be made from clay." Now I know the meaning of *clay*.

Tell children about additional dictionary features. Some words have more than one definition. When there is more than one definition, try each definition in the sentence and choose the one that makes the most sense. Many dictionaries also give information about how to say a word and how to use it in a sentence.

Mini-Lesson 1

Remind children that...
- a dictionary is a book with a list of words and their meanings.
- dictionaries can help us learn new words.

Word List

barn	milk
corn	puppy
doll	sheep
giraffe	tree
house	window

Guide Practice

Write the sentence *I saw a giraffe at the zoo.* Underline *giraffe*. This is the word *giraffe*. Let's look in a dictionary for the meaning of the word *giraffe*. If possible, use an illustrated dictionary.

- What is the first letter of the word *giraffe*? (*g*) That's

right. I will go to the *g* section of the dictionary. Have a child volunteer help you find the word.

- Do you see a picture next to the word *giraffe*? (yes) What does it look like? (Possible response: It is an animal that has spots and a long neck.)
- The definition says "a large African mammal that has a very long neck and spotted skin." Does this meaning make sense in the sentence *I saw a giraffe at the zoo*? (yes)

Follow the same procedure with other words from the Word List.

If... children have difficulty looking up words, **then...** review how to use a dictionary in Lesson 9.

On Their Own Help children complete Worktext p. 82.

Mini-Lesson 2

Remind children that...

- a *dictionary* is a book with a list of words and their meanings.
- dictionaries can help us figure out the correct meaning of words that have more than one meaning.

Word List

bit	over
calf	room
check	report
feet	still
letter	trunk

Guide Practice

Write the sentence *Pam's left calf hurt.* Read it and underline the word *calf.* I know that a calf is a baby cow, but that meaning does not make sense here. This word must have more than one meaning. To find the other meaning, we are going to look in a dictionary.

- What is the first letter of *calf*? (*c*) Yes, let's look in c section for the word *calf.*
- What is a meaning other than "baby cow"? ("the part of the leg below the knee and behind the shin")
- Does this meaning make sense in the sentence? (yes)

When a word has more than one meaning, try each meaning in the sentence and choose the meaning that makes the most sense. Repeat the procedure with the other words from the Word List.

If... children have difficulty looking up words, **then...** review Lesson 9 to learn how to use a dictionary.

On Their Own Assign Worktext p. 83.

Mini-Lesson 3

Remind children that...

- dictionaries can help us learn the meanings of new words.
- dictionaries list all definitions for a word, and they also show how to say and use a word.

Word List

annoy	odd
blossom	show
branch	sign
clump	station
field	wind

Guide Practice

Write the word *wind.* How do you say this word, and what does it mean? Children will likely pronounce the word and give the definition of *wind* as in "moving air." Is *wind* a thing or an action? (thing)

Then write *Does the river wind through the forest?* Underline *wind.*

- Read aloud the sentence, replacing "wind" with "moving air." Does "moving air" make sense in the sentence? (no)
- In this sentence, *wind* is an action word, and it's pronounced differently. A dictionary tells you how to say it. Work with children to find *wind* in a dictionary. Point to the pronunciation key, pronounce the word correctly, and have students repeat after you.
- What are some meanings of *wind*? ("turn something," "move with twists and turns," "end")
- Try each meaning in the sentence. Which one makes the most sense? ("move with twists and turns") Repeat the process with the other words in the Word List.

If... children have difficulty reading the pronunciation symbols, **then...** walk them through a pronunciation key.

On Their Own Assign Worktext p. 84.

Introduce to children the concept of context clues. Sometimes when we read a new word, we can figure out the meaning of the word from other words in the sentence or passage.

Teach children how words can be defined within a sentence. Write and read aloud: *We did a splendid, or really great, job.* Underline *splendid.* The definition of this word, *splendid,* is in the sentence: "really great." Underline *really great.* This definition doesn't need to sound like it came out of a dictionary. It just needs to say what the word means in the sentence. Point to and circle *or.* The word *or* is a clue word. This word tells me that a meaning is about to be given.

Write *My beagle, a small dog, loves to play ball.* In other sentences, words or phrases right next to a word tell more about the word. Circle *a small dog.* This phrase renames, or gives other words for, the word *beagle.* It tells me that a beagle is a kind of dog. Point to the commas in the sentence. Sometimes the words between commas tell about the word before or after them.

Write *pear* and *pair.* Some words, like *pair* and *pear,* sound the same but have different meanings. When I read the word *pear,* I can figure out its meaning by paying attention to other words in the sentence. Write *Pears and grapes are my favorite fruits. Grapes* and *fruit* are clue words. This spelling of *pear* must mean "a kind of fruit." Even if I had never heard the word *pear* before, I could figure out its meaning from these clues.

MATERIALS
Worktext pp. 85–87

Mini-Lesson 1

Remind children that...
- paying attention to all the words in a sentence can help us learn new words.
- sometimes a word's meaning is given within a sentence.

Word List

absent	excellent
aid	fasten
author	grumble
bawl	leaps
champion	purchase

Guide Practice
Write the sentence *Jack leaps, or jumps, to catch the ball.* Read the sentence aloud and underline *leaps.* This is the word *leaps.* Say it with me: *leaps.* Is the meaning of *leaps* given in this sentence? (yes) What does *leaps* mean? (jumps) What is the clue word? *(or)* Follow the same

procedure with other words from the Word Lists. For sentences without the clue word *or,* ask children, "What words are in between the commas? What word do those words tell about? What do you think the word means?"

Other possible example sentences include the following: *My mom will <u>purchase</u>, or buy, a new TV. The movie was <u>excellent</u>, or great.*

If... children have difficulty understanding how the phrases can help them,
then... read the sentences without those words. Then read the complete sentence again and discuss the clues that the words give to the reader.

On Their Own Read aloud the directions and sentences on Worktext p. 85 and assign the page.

Mini-Lesson 2

Remind children that...

- some words sound the same but have different spellings and meanings.
- clue words in a sentence can show us which meaning is correct.

Word List

so	herd
sew	meat
knot	meet
not	pear
heard	pair

Guide Practice

Help children use context clues to understand the meanings of homophones. Write *We won the game by two points.* Below it write *I have one sister.* Underline *won* and *one. Won* and *one* sound the same, but they have different meanings. Read the first sentence with children.

- What does *won* mean in this sentence? (got a higher
- What words helped you figure out the meaning of *won* (game, points)
- Does this meaning of *won* make sense in the second sentence? (no)
- What does *one* mean when it is spelled *o, n, e*? (a number)

Follow the same procedure with the other words from the Word List. Possible example sentences include the following: *I'll meet you after school; Burgers are my favorite kind of meat.*

If... children have difficulty recognizing clue words, **then...** clarify the meaning of each homophone by asking questions such as, "What does it mean to win? What is something you can win?"

On Their Own With children, read through the directions and each sentences on Worktext p. 86. Direct children to complete the page.

Mini-Lesson 3

Remind children that...

- clue words in a sentence can help us figure out the meanings of unfamiliar words.
- clue words also appear in sentences surrounding the unfamiliar word.

Word List

beware	examine
bold	grasp
clever	injure
dart	mention
delay	oppose

Guide Practice

Write and read aloud: *The sign on the gate said to beware of the dog. It had a picture of a large dog that looked angry.*

- Underline *beware.* I want to know what *beware* means. What detail in the second sentence gives me a clue? *(large dog that looks angry)*
- What do you think is the meaning of *beware*? (Possible response: "watch out for")

Follow the same procedure with these sentences: *Annie was bold. She went on her first roller coaster ride without feeling afraid.*

If... children have difficulty identifying the clues, **then...** help them locate one clue, and ask for examples of other clues that support the same meaning.

On Their Own Have children complete Worktext p. 87.

Introduce to children the concept of word structure. When you come across a word you don't know, it is helpful to look at the parts of the word. Looking at the parts of the word can help you understand the word.

Model for students how to read words with word endings. Write *raining.* The word *raining* has more than one part. To read the word *raining,* first I figure out the base word. A *base word* is a word without any added word parts. **Cover** *ing* with your hand and read the base word *rain.* The base word of *raining* is *rain.* **Cover** *rain.* The word *raining* has the word ending *-ing.* I see this ending on lots of words for actions, like *running, jumping,* and *playing.* Now I am going to read the base word and the word ending together: *rain, -ing, raining.* A sentence with this word is *It is raining outside.*

Show students how to decode a word by looking at its prefix or suffix. Write *helpful.* This is the word *helpful.* The word *helpful* has a suffix, or a word part added to the end. **Point to** *ful.* The suffix *-ful* means "full of." **Cover** *ful.* To read this word, first I find the base word: *help.* Then I read the base word and the suffix together: *help, -ful, helpful.* **Run your hand below the word parts as you read the word.** The word *helpful* means "full of help." If I add the prefix *un-* to this word, I have the word *unhelpful.* The prefix *un-* means "the opposite of" or "not." The word *unhelpful* means "not helpful."

MATERIALS
Worktext pp. 88–90

Mini-Lesson 1

Remind children that...
- understanding word parts helps us learn new words.
- some words have word endings such as *-ed* or *-ing.*

Word List

eat	jumped
eating	jumping
help	look
helping	looked
jump	looking

Guide Practice
Guide children in recognizing word parts. Write *eating, jumping, helping,* and *looking.*

- Point to *eating.* What shorter word do you see? (*eat*) Yes, *eat* is the base word. The word ending *-ing* was added to *eat.* Read aloud *eating* and have children repeat after you.

- Repeat the procedure with the other words. Then pantomime eating, jumping, and looking. Ask children what you are doing with each motion. The words *eating, jumping,* and *looking* sound alike. These words end with the ending *-ing.*

Repeat this process with the remaining words from the Word Lists. Then model adding *-ed* instead of *-ing* to form the words *jumped* and *looked.* Once children understand the words, explain that the ending *-ed* tells that an action already happened. The ending *-ing* tells that an action is happening now or happens regularly.

If... children have difficulty identifying the ending *-ing,* **then...** repeat the process with other words, such as *singing, talking,* and *walking.*

On Their Own Help children complete Worktext p. 88.

Mini-Lesson 2

Remind children that...
- understanding word parts helps us learn new words.
- identifying the base word is the first step in reading words with prefixes and suffixes.

Word List

longer	preheat
longest	prepay
overeat	preschool
overload	younger
overpay	youngest

Guide Practice

Guide children to read and understand words with prefixes and suffixes. Write *preheat*. The word *preheat* has the prefix *pre-*. *Pre-* means "before." **Cover** *pre.* Ask children to identify the base word. Then ask them to tell the meaning of the word and use it in a sentence. Follow the same procedure with the words *preschool, prepay,*

overpay, overload, and *overeat.* Inform children that prefix *over-* means "too much."

Write *longer* and *longest*. Draw three lines to represent *long, longer,* and *longest*. The words *longer* and *longest* both have suffixes. The suffix *-er* means "more." The suffix *-est* means "most." *Longer* and *longest* have the same base word. What is it? (**long**) What does *longer* mean? (**more long**) What does *longest* mean? (**most long**) Which line is longest? (**Children should direct you to the longest line.**)

If... children have difficulty understanding the meanings of the words,

then... have them say the base word first and then add the meaning of the prefix (e.g., *overload* means "load too much").

On Their Own Have children complete Worktext p. 89.

Mini-Lesson 3

Remind children that...
- looking at word parts separately helps us read new words.
- *compound words* are two small words put together.

Word List

bathroom	peaceful
fearless	fearful
flagpole	sleepless
hopeful	snowball
hopeless	weekend

Guide Practice

Write *hopeful*. You know that the suffix *-ful* means "full of." What is the base word of *hopeful?* (**hope**) What does this word mean? (**"full of hope"**) The word *hopeless* also has the base word *hope*. What suffix does *hopeless* have? (**-less**) The suffix *-less* means "without." What does the word *hopeless* mean? (**"without hope"**)

Then model how to look at the word structure of compound words. Write *doorbell*. The word *doorbell* is made of two small words: *door* and *bell*. The two parts of this word can help me understand the word's meaning. A *door* is a way to get into a house. A *bell* is something that makes noise. A *doorbell* is a bell that goes on a door. Words like *doorbell* are called *compound words*.

Guide children to look at word parts to find the meanings of the remaining words on the Word Lists.

If... children have difficulty defining words with prefixes and suffixes,

then... prompt students using words and the meaning of the prefixes or suffixes: *Hopeless* means without _____.

On Their Own Have children complete Worktext p. 90.

Vocabulary
Student Worktext

1. Where are you?

2. Come here.

3. What is that?

4. Help me please.

5. My little dog ran away.

6. Your horse is big.

7. Many ducks are in the park.

8. He said to go that way.

 Directions Read one of the sentences aloud. Have your child find the sentence you read. Then have your child read a sentence aloud for you to find.

where	come
what	help
little	your
many	said

1. Where could the bus be?

2. Read the paper.

3. Many people eat here.

4. Where do you live?

5. There is a bird in the nest.

6. My parents work there.

7. We could play together.

8. Is there any food?

Directions Help your child cut up a sentence into individual words. Have your child read each word to you in random order. Then have your child put the words back together to make the sentence. Have him or her read it aloud. Repeat with other sentences.

could

paper

people

live

there

work

together

food

1. My kitten will grow.

2. It will become big.

3. I always go to this store.

4. Sam and I go around the park.

5. Where is the water?

6. There are three people in his family.

7. I saw their team.

8. There were three people.

 School +Home **Directions** Point to a word in one of the sentences. Have your child read the word to you. Repeat with other words.

grow	become
always	around
water	family
their	were

1. Sam has nothing to do.

2. We want everything to grow.

3. Pam has enough paper.

4. She has her own puppy.

5. The puppy lives at her house.

6. I like to go to school.

7. Sam and Pam go every day.

8. Our game is fun.

 Directions Choose a word in one of the sentences. Have your child find that word written some place else, such as in the newspaper, in a magazine, or on a food container. Then have your child read the word to you.

nothing	everything
enough	own
house	school
every	our

1. My friends are in the house.

2. The kitten is afraid of the water.

3. Mom and I read every day.

4. We want to play it again.

5. I know what I want to eat.

6. The food is done.

7. Where does your family live?

8. She said goodbye to her friends.

Directions Help your child cut up the words in one of the sentences. Have your child put the words back together to make the sentence. Then have your child read the sentence to you. Repeat with other sentences.

friends

afraid

read

again

know

done

does

goodbye

1. They eat before school.

2. The rabbit won't go near the house.

3. You are right.

4. Won't that be a surprise!

5. Would you come to my house?

6. Do not worry.

7. Do you think about your cat?

8. I can read the sign.

 Directions Secretly choose a word in one of the sentences. Spell the word aloud slowly. Have your child find the word and read it to you. Repeat with other words. Then have your child read the sentences aloud.

Vocabulary Lesson 1

before

won't

right

surprise

would

worry

about

sign

1. All my friends like to draw.

2. I touch the flower.

3. Sam and I draw with many colors.

4. I draw the sky above water.

5. I have a great surprise for you.

6. My father likes to draw pictures.

7. We eat together once a day.

8. They found enough food to eat.

 Directions Help your child cut up the sentences into individual words. Lay the words face down. Have your child pick words one at a time and read them to you.

draw

touch

colors

above

great

pictures

once

found

Name _____

1. My dad took me to school.

2. I laugh with my friends.

3. We thought that it would rain.

4. Do you remember me?

5. I only have a blue mat.

6. My school is across from my house.

7. Sam ran because of the rain.

8. I opened the paper.

 School + Home **Directions** Say a word from one of the sentences and have your child spell it for you. Repeat with other words.

took

laugh

thought

remember

only

across

because

opened

1. My mom put on her shoes.

2. Her friends were behind the house.

3. They came toward the house.

4. We opened the door.

5. Pam has brown eyes.

6. She loved the surprise.

7. We sat among our friends.

8. I want this room instead of that one.

Directions Have your child copy the sentences on a separate piece of paper. Then have your child read the sentences to you.

Vocabulary Lesson 1

Name _____

shoes

behind

toward

door

eyes

loved

among

instead

1. Can I get another room?

2. None of them said goodbye.

3. He goes to school every day.

4. It is too early to go to school.

5. He leans against the door.

6. The door is heavy.

7. I have a surprise for you today.

8. What should I do now?

Directions Write a word from the sentences on paper, in large letters. Have your child outline the letters of the word several times. Ask your child to name each letter as it is outlined and then read the word. Repeat with other words.

Vocabulary Lesson 1

another	**none**
goes	**early**
against	**heavy**
today	**should**

1. He lives in a different country.

2. The people built a new house.

3. I like to learn in school.

4. My sister wants to read about science.

5. The children ran through the house.

6. No one answered the door.

7. The flowers are beautiful.

8. All the flowers are different colors.

Directions Read one of the sentences aloud. Have your child find the sentence you read. Then have your child read a sentence for you to find.

Vocabulary Lesson 1

country

built

learn

science

through

answered

beautiful

different

Name _____

1. Someone please answer the door.

2. My shoes are somewhere in the house.

3. I have looked everywhere.

4. There is a sign above the machines.

5. Could you please move this heavy sign?

6. Would you like to go around the world?

7. Sam and Pam could build a house.

8. They couldn't be late for school.

 Directions Have your child cut up a few of the sentences into individual words. Have your child read each word to you in random order.

Vocabulary Lesson 1

someone	somewhere
everywhere	machines
move	world
build	couldn't

1. My friends are gone.

2. How many animals do you see?

3. We often come here.

4. I cut my food in little pieces.

5. Dad likes the house though it is small.

6. Do not break the machines.

7. I heard someone at the door.

8. Listen to what your mother said.

Directions Randomly point to a word in one of the sentences. Have your child read the word to you. Repeat with other words.

gone

animals

often

pieces

though

break

heard

listen

Name _____

1. Either one is good to eat.

2. That storm was the worst.

3. You're very good at science.

4. Our whole family lives here.

5. My friend bought toys for the cats.

6. My mother brought me to school.

7. Everybody made new friends.

8. Please wait here for one minute.

 Directions Choose a word in one of the sentences. Have your child find that word written someplace else, such as in the newspaper, in a magazine, or on a food container. Then have your child read the word to you.

Vocabulary Lesson 1

either

worst

you're

whole

bought

brought

everybody

minute

1. We finally found my little dog!

2. Where have you been?

3. I guess he was in the park.

4. I believe you are right.

5. My friend caught a cold.

6. Will you go to school tomorrow?

7. There is only a half day of school.

8. Our neighbor moved to a different house.

 Directions Write a word from the sentences in large letters on paper. Have your child outline the letters of the word several times. Ask your child to name each letter as it is outlined and then read the word. Repeat with other words.

finally

been

guess

believe

caught

tomorrow

half

neighbor

1. Her parents want to buy a new house.

2. They have four daughters in their family.

3. I am the youngest in my family.

4. My mother bought me new clothes.

5. I am in school for eight hours every day.

6. She has money for a new book.

7. Can I ask you a question?

8. Who taught you about animals?

School + Home **Directions** Say a word from one of the sentences and have your child spell it for you.

buy

daughters

youngest

clothes

hours

money

question

taught

Name _____

Name each picture.
Color the farm animals red.
Color the zoo animals green.
Color the pets blue.

Animals

School + Home **Directions** In school, your child sorted these pictures into three groups—Zoo Animals, Pets, and Farm Animals. Have your child name each picture and explain which group it goes into. Then ask your child to name another animal for each group.

34 Classify and Categorize

Vocabulary Lesson 2

Name _____

Name each picture.
Draw lines between things that are like each other.

Clothes

T-shirt

shorts

cap

pants

sweater

ski hat

School + Home

Directions In school, your child sorted these pictures into groups. Have your child name each picture and tell you why it is like another picture. Pictures can be grouped by use or weather. There is not one correct answer.

Vocabulary Lesson 2

Classify and Categorize **35**

Name _____

Name each picture.
Draw a line from each picture to something like it.

Ways to Go

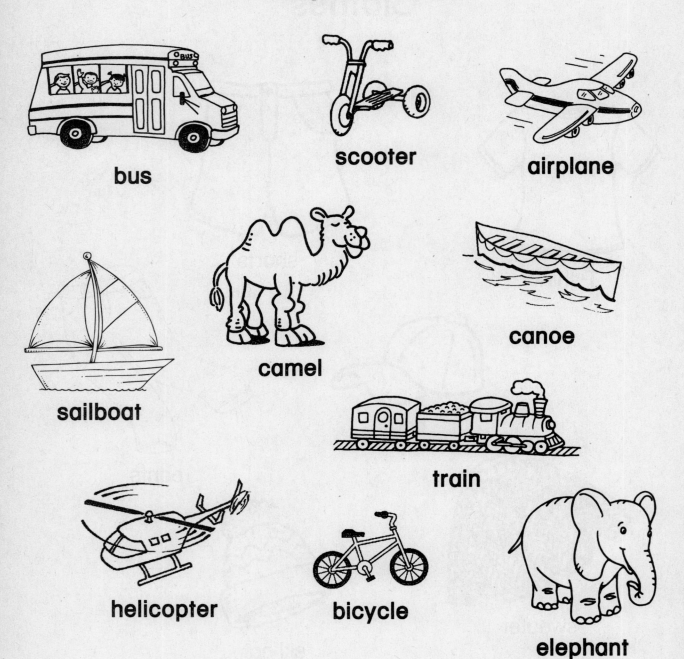

bus

scooter

airplane

sailboat

camel

canoe

train

helicopter

bicycle

elephant

Directions In school, your child looked for ways to connect these pictures of ways to travel. Have your child name each picture and explain which other picture or pictures are like it. Then ask your child to name something else that could go with those pictures. There is more than one way to group the pictures.

36 Classify and Categorize

Vocabulary Lesson 2

Name _____

Cut out the pictures.
Name the pictures.
Put the pictures in order.

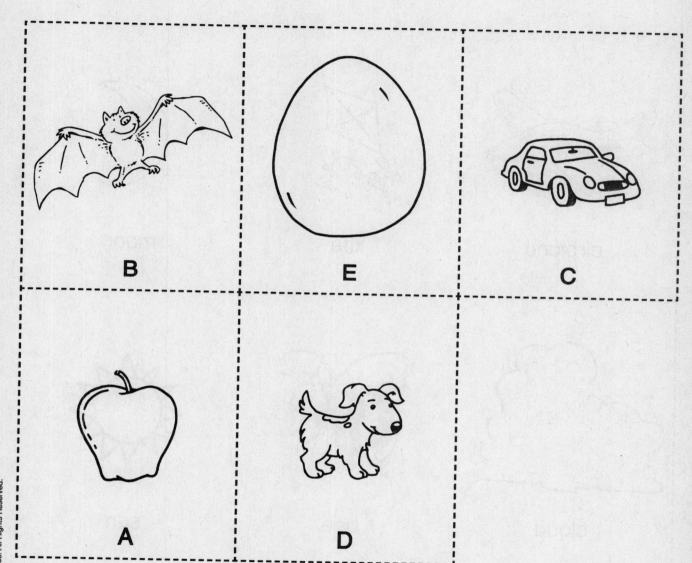

B

E

C

A

D

Directions Help your child name each picture: *bat, apple, egg, dog,* and *car.* Ask your child to identify the first letter in each word. Then help him or her put the pictures in *ABC* order.

Vocabulary Lesson 3

Alphabetize **37**

Name _____

Cut out the pictures.
Name the pictures.
Put the pictures in *ABC* order.

airplane

kite

moon

cloud

bee

sun

Directions In school, your child learned about putting words in alphabetical order. Help your child read the words and name the first letter of each word. Then ask him or her to put the words in alphabetical order.

Vocabulary Lesson 3

Read the words. **Put** them in alphabetical order.
Draw a line to the correct spot.
Rewrite the words.

1. Monday

2. Tuesday

3. Wednesday

4. Thursday

5. Friday

6. Saturday

7. Sunday

Directions Help your child read the words and name the first letters of each word. Ask him or her to put the words in alphabetical order.

Name _____

Look at the pictures.
Say the words.

 School + Home

Directions In school, your child learned about compound words. Help your child identify the pictures: *backpack, playground, goldfish, baseball,* and *teapot.* Say each word for your child so he or she can hear the two small words within each word. Then talk with your child about what each word means.

Vocabulary Lesson 4

Name _____

Read the words. **Cut** out the word boxes.
Put the word in the correct box.

```
┌ ─ ─ ─ ─ ┬ ─ ─ ─ ─ ┬ ─ ─ ─ ─ ┬ ─ ─ ─ ─ ┬ ─ ─ ─ ─ ┐
│ campfire │ toothbrush │ popcorn │ seashell │ mailbox │
└ ─ ─ ─ ─ ┴ ─ ─ ─ ─ ┴ ─ ─ ─ ─ ┴ ─ ─ ─ ─ ┴ ─ ─ ─ ─ ┘
```

1. mail + box =

2. sea + shell =

3. tooth + brush =

4. camp + fire =

5. pop + corn =

School + Home

Directions In school, your child matched compound words to the small words within the compound words. Read each compound word with your child. Take turns using the words in sentences.

Name _____

Read the underlined compound word in each sentence.
Find the two small words in each compound word.
Use one of these small words to finish the sentence.

1. We can get _____ by reading the <u>newspaper</u>.

2. Joe will take a _____ in the <u>bathtub</u>.

3. Kate likes to _____ on her <u>skateboard</u>.

4. The _____ is in the <u>fireplace</u>.

5. The _____ is on the <u>bookshelf</u>.

6. We use _____ to make a <u>snowman</u>.

Directions Help your child find the two small words in each compound word. Ask your child which of the small words best completes each sentence. Then have your child write the word on the line and read aloud the sentence.

School + Home

Vocabulary Lesson 4

Color the pictures.
Talk about the pictures.

Directions In school, your child learned to describe objects using words for colors and numbers. Ask your child to color the pictures and describe them. For example, your child can tell you how many of each clothing item they see.

Name _____

Read each word. **Cut** out the words.
Color the picture.
Talk about the picture. **Use** the words.

| five | six | seven | eight | nine | ten |

Directions Ask your child to color this picture and then describe it using words for numbers and colors. Then ask him or her to use the number cards to describe things in your home.

44 Descriptive Words: Numbers and Color

Vocabulary Lesson 5

Name _____

Read each word. **Cut** out the words.
Put the words in the correct order.
Color the picture.
Talk about the picture.

| twenty | thirty | forty | fifty | sixty |

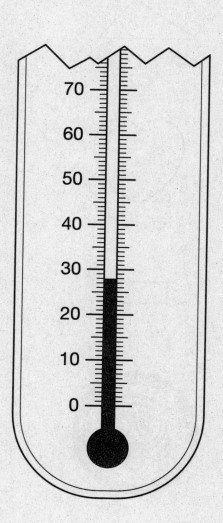

Directions Ask your child to read the number words and describe the picture. Then talk with your child about how the weather feels at each of the temperatures.

Vocabulary Lesson 5   Descriptive Words: Numbers and Color **45**

Name _____

Look at the pictures.
Talk about the pictures.

1.

2.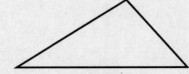

3.

4.

5.

Vocabulary Lesson 6

Name _____

Color the picture cards. **Cut** out the picture cards.
Choose one picture card. **Do not let** your partner see it.
Describe the fruit. **Do not name** the fruit.

 School + Home

Directions Have your child choose one fruit to describe to you without naming it. Guess which fruit your child is describing. Encourage your child to give you as much detail as possible.

Vocabulary Lesson 6   Descriptive Words: Size, Shape, and Texture **47**

Name _____

Cut out the picture cards.
Choose one picture card. **Do not let** your partner see it.
Describe the animal. **Do not name** the animal.

48 Descriptive Words: Size, Shape, and Texture

Vocabulary Lesson 6

Draw a picture of a family having a picnic.
Talk about your picture.

Directions Have your child draw a picture of a gathering around the table and then describe it in detail. Ask your child to tell you who is in the picture, where they are, and what they are doing. Encourage him or her to include many details.

Name _____

Choose one object. **Draw** a picture of yourself using it.
Talk about your picture. **Use** the words **first, then, after,** and **last.**

School + Home

Name _____

Cut out the pictures. **Make** a picture of a celebration.
Talk about your picture.

Directions Have your child use these pictures to make a picture of a celebration.
Then ask your child to tell you about the celebration. Encourage him or her to use
as much detail as possible.

Name _____

Read the days of the week.
Pick a day. **Draw** what you did.
Talk about your day.

Monday	Tuesday	Wednesday	Thursday	Friday	Saturday	Sunday

Directions In school, your child talked about the days of the week using words for time order, such as *first*, *next*, and *last*. Read the days of the week with your child. Then ask your child to explain his or her picture.

Vocabulary Lesson 8

Read the words.
Cut out the word cards.

first	then	tomorrow	during
later	next	after	today
before	yesterday	now	last

Directions In school, your child learned words for time and order. Read the word cards with your child. Take turns picking a card and using the word in a sentence. Then ask your child to use at least three of the words to tell you about something that happened this week.

Name _____

Read the passage.
Cut out the words.
Fill in the blanks.

Summer begins in _____. In the summer, I wake up

early in the _____. I _____ my day by

eating breakfast. When I _____ breakfast, I like to go

to the pool. I like to swim and go down the slide _____

I am at the pool. Later, in the _____, my friend John

comes over to watch movies. When we _____ the

movie, it is _____ time to go to bed.

June	evening	begin	finish

finish	finally	while	morning

School + Home **Directions** In school, your child learned words for time and order. Read the paragraph with your child. Ask him or her which word correctly fills in each blank.

Vocabulary Lesson 8

Look up each word in a dictionary.
Draw a picture to show the thing.

anteater	bib
bicycle	zipper

Directions Have your child look up words in the dictionary and then illustrate them. Ask your child to tell you the meaning of each word.

School + Home

Name _____

Circle the guide words for each entry word.

Entry Word	Guide Words	
1. believe	bare / base	bean / beside
2. hunter	humble / hurt	hip / hop
3. blizzard	blink / boy	bark / best
4. nail	nab / name	nine / none
5. afternoon	add / adult	afraid / again

School + Home **Directions** Have your child identify the guide words for these entry words. Ask your child to show you how he or she chose the correct guide words.

56 Dictionary/Glossary

Vocabulary Lesson 9

Name _____ **57**

Read each word and its meaning.
Write one word on each line to finish the sentence.

catch to grab a moving thing

under below

few not many

surprise something not expected

_____

1. Our parents always have a _____ for us on holidays.

2. The book fell _____ the table.

3. Can you _____ the ball?

4. Only a _____ people came to school today.

Directions In school, your child learned about phrases in a dictionary that can illustrate the meaning of a word. Read the meanings and phrases with your child. Have him or her tell you which word completes each phrase. Then have your child use each word above in his or her own sentence.

Make two groups with the pictures.
Color one group red and one group blue.

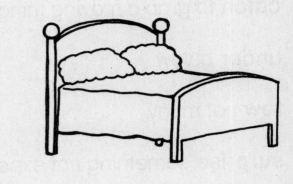

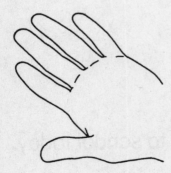

Directions In school, your child sorted these pictures into two groups—a group of like things and a group of things not in that group. Have your child tell you how he or she sorted the pictures. Then ask your child to color the pictures based on the groups he or she made. Ask your child to draw another picture and tell you to which group it belongs.

Vocabulary Lesson 10

Name _____

Read the words.
Circle the pictures that go together.

eight

five

pencil

sign

horse

nine

chair

two

Directions In school, your child discussed how to sort these pictures into two groups—a group of like things and a group of things not in that group. Have your child circle the pictures that go together. Then have your child tell you how he or she sorted the pictures into groups.

Vocabulary Lesson 10

Sort Words: Two Categories **59**

Name _____

Read the words.
Cut out the words.
Sort the words into two groups.

| ladder | eagle | garden | robin |
| fifteen | cracker | parrot | rooster |

Group 1 | # Group 2

Directions In school, your child learned about sorting words into two groups—a group of like things and a group of things not in that group. Have your child sort the words into groups and tell you how he or she sorted the words.

Vocabulary Lesson 10

Name _____

Cut out the picture cards.
Sort them into groups.

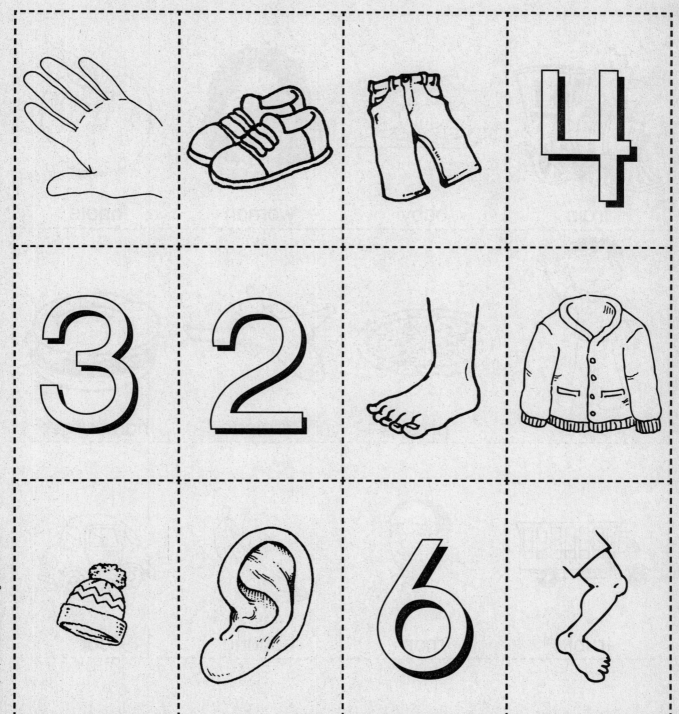

Directions In school, your child discussed how to sort these pictures into groups. Have your child sort the pictures for you. Ask your child to tell you why he or she put the pictures into groups.

Vocabulary Lesson 11   Sort Words: Multiple Categories   **61**

Name _____

Cut out the picture cards.
Sort them into groups.

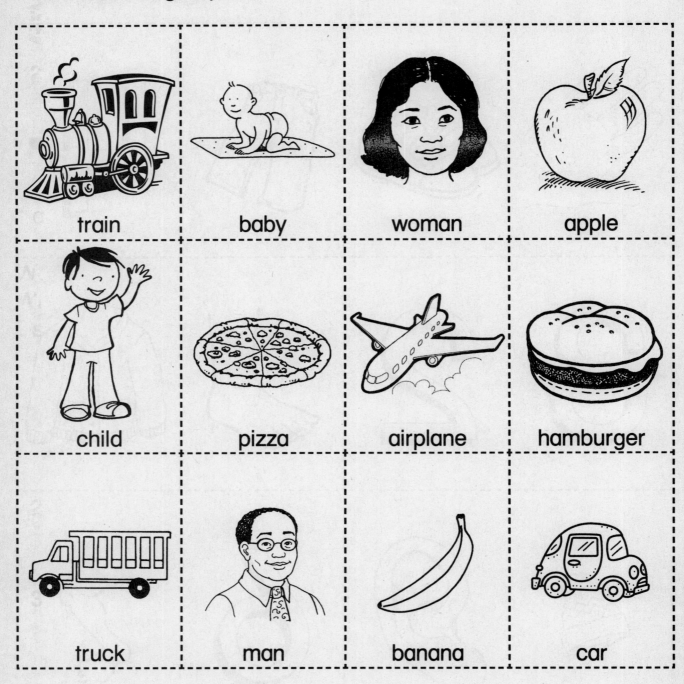

train	baby	woman	apple
child	pizza	airplane	hamburger
truck	man	banana	car

Directions In school, your child discussed how to sort these pictures into groups.
Have your child sort the pictures for you. Ask your child to tell you why he or she put
the pictures into groups.

Vocabulary Lesson 11

Name _____   **63**

Read the words.
Draw a line between words that go together.
Name another word that goes in each group.

mustard   uncle

aunt   basement

kitchen   ketchup

radio   May

April   television

Directions Have your child connect the words in each column to form groups. Have your child name the pairs of words and say how they are alike. Then ask them to name another word that goes in each group.

Name _____

Read the sentences.
Underline the definition of the bold word.

1. The **ewe,** a girl sheep, was big.

2. Matt saw **trout,** a kind of fish, in the lake.

3. My sister's **crib,** a bed for a baby, is soft.

4. Helen has a pet **chick,** or baby hen.

5. Our dog likes to **stare,** or look, at cats.

6. Jen's play pen has a **gate,** or door.

School + Home **Directions** In school, your child learned how to figure out meanings of words by looking for definitions in the sentences. Read the sentences with your child. Ask your child to show you the definition for each bold word.

Vocabulary Lesson 12

Read each sentence.
Circle the clue word that introduces the examples.
Underline the examples.

1. Sara packed **supplies,** such as a flashlight and juice boxes, for the trip.

2. Many **creatures,** such as raccoons and bats, come out at night.

3. The clown did **stunts**—for example, he rode a tiny bike!

4. Lisa bought camping **gear,** like a tent and sleeping bag.

5. We visited **attractions,** such as the park and museum.

6. Are there danger **warnings,** like flashing lights or whistles?

School + Home

Directions In school, your child learned how an example can explain the meaning of an unfamiliar word in a sentence. Read each sentence with your child. Then take turns using the examples to explain what each bold word means.

Name _____

Read each sentence.
Circle the clue words.
Underline the synonym or antonym.

1. Jill was **exhausted,** and Kendra was tired too.

2. That house is **gigantic,** but this one is small.

3. She **revealed** her secret, and I told my secret too.

4. Alex **chuckled,** and the old man laughed quietly too.

5. Sandra **remembered** to come, but Mari forgot.

6. That dog acts **wild,** but this dog is calm.

School + Home **Directions** In school, your child learned how to use synonyms or antonyms to figure out the meaning of a word in a sentence. Read each sentence with your child. Then help your child use the antonyms or synonyms to figure out the meaning of each bold word.

Name _____

Write ly after each word.
Draw a picture that shows what the word means.

nice_____	loud_____
sad_____	neat_____

Directions Read each word with your child. Have your child draw pictures to express the words *nicely*, *loudly*, *sadly*, and *neatly*. Ask your child to explain his or her pictures. Encourage your child to use the *-ly* words on the page in a sentence.

Name _____

Write ly after each word.
Write the new word on the line.
Use the clues to finish the puzzle.

1. kind _____ _____ _____

2. fair _____ _____ _____

3. wild _____ _____ _____

	1.		
2. f		k		r	l	
		n	
3. w			d		
		y	

Directions Have your child complete the puzzle. Ask your child to make up sentences that include the words on the page. Then ask your child to name other words he or she can think of that end in *-ly*.

Name _____

Read each word.
Write ly at the end of each word.
Write the new word on the line in the sentence.

1. sweet _____

   _ _ _ _ _

   The baby smiled _____.

2. light _____

   _ _ _ _ _

   She tapped _____ on the door.

3. sudden _____

   _ _ _ _ _

   The bus stopped _____.

4. brave _____

   _ _ _ _ _

   Paul _____ swam across the river.

Directions Have your child add the suffix -ly to each word and write the word in the sentence. Read the words and sentences with your child. Then ask your child to tell you what each word means.

Name _____

Name each picture.
Draw a line between pictures that have the same name.

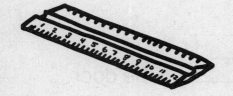

Copyright © Pearson Education, Inc., or its affiliates. All Rights Reserved.

 School + Home **Directions** Have your child pair the pictures that share a name. Then ask him or her to name each picture and use the word in a sentence.

Vocabulary Lesson 14

Name _____

Read the words.
Circle the words that go with the picture.

1. baseball cap   toothpaste cap

2. light bulb   onion bulb

3. city block   toy block

4. window shade   tree shade

5. flower bed   soft bed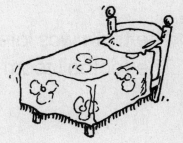

School + Home **Directions** Help your child complete the page. Then read the phrases with your child and take turns using the phrases in a sentence.

Name _____

Read the sentences.
Underline the word that is the same in each pair of sentences.
Draw a line from the picture to the correct sentence.

1. James put money in his **bank**.
   Peter fished by the **bank** of the river.

2. Jill got new books as a **present**.
   There's no time like the **present**.

3. The **train** was late getting to the railroad station.
   The football team has to **train** before the game.

Directions Your child learned to look at clue words in sentences to decide which meaning is the right one for words with more than one meaning. Have your child tell you what each multiple-meaning word means in these sentences.

Name _____

Read each word.
Add re or **un** at the beginning of each word.
Write the new word on the line.

1. do

   un

   _____   _____

   _ _ _ _ _ _   _ _ _ _ _ _ _ _ _ _ _ _ _
   _____ do   _____

   re

   _____   _____

   _ _ _ _ _ _   _ _ _ _ _ _ _ _ _ _ _ _ _
   _____ do   _____

2. tie

   un

   _____   _____

   _ _ _ _ _ _   _ _ _ _ _ _ _ _ _ _ _ _ _
   _____ tie   _____

   re

   _____   _____

   _ _ _ _ _ _   _ _ _ _ _ _ _ _ _ _ _ _ _
   _____ tie   _____

3. pin

   un

   _____   _____

   _ _ _ _ _ _   _ _ _ _ _ _ _ _ _ _ _ _ _
   _____ pin   _____

4. paint

   re

   _____   _____

   _ _ _ _ _ _   _ _ _ _ _ _ _ _ _ _ _ _ _
   _____ paint   _____

Directions Have your child add the prefixes *un-* and *re-* to the words. Read the words with your child, and then take turns making up sentences for each of the word.

Name _____

Add the prefix to the base word.
Write the new word on the line.

1. **dis** + like _____

2. **dis** + obey _____

3. **dis** + agree _____

4. **mis** + use _____

5. **mis** + spell _____

6. **mis** + match _____

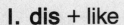 **Directions** Have your child add the prefixes *dis-* and *mis-* to the words. Read the words with your child, and then take turns making up sentences for each of the word.

Circle the prefix.
Underline the base word.
Write the base word on the line to finish the sentence.

1. *Impatient* means not _____.

2. *Imperfect* means not _____.

3. *Indefinite* means not _____.

4. *Incorrect* means not _____.

5. *Impolite* means not _____.

6. *Informal* means not _____.

Directions In school, your child read words with the prefixes *im-* and *in-*. Help your child use some of these words in sentences.

Name _____

Look at the picture.
Draw a circle around the word that goes with it.

1.  hot cold	2.  dry wet
3.  soft hard	4.  happy sad
5.  sweet sour	6.  heavy light

Vocabulary Lesson 16

Name _____

Look at the picture. **Draw** the opposite next to it.
Write the opposite word next to your drawing.

I.	big cat		_____ - - - - - - _____ **cat**
2.	empty glass		_____ - - - - - - _____ **glass**
3.	narrow door		_____ - - - - - - _____ **door**
4.	thick line		_____ - - - - - - _____ **line**
5.	high sock		_____ - - - - - - _____ **sock**

low	thin	small	full	wide

Directions In school, your child learned about words with opposite meanings.
Read each pair of opposites. Then help your child think of another pair of opposites
and ask him or her to draw pictures of the words and act them out.

Name _____

Read the words. **Cut** out the cards.
Match the words for opposites.

always	up	sick
asleep	young	old
healthy	awake	here
never	down	there

 Directions In school, your child learned about words with opposite meanings. Read each pair of opposites. Then help your child think of another pair of opposites and ask him or her to draw pictures of the words and act them out.

Name _____

Look at the pictures. **Move** each word next to its picture.
Read the words.

| small   grass   slacks   picture   rip   chair |

little

_____
_ _ _ _ _ _ _ _ _ _ _ _ _ _ _ _ _ _ _
_____

drawing

_____
_ _ _ _ _ _ _ _ _ _ _ _ _ _ _ _ _ _ _
_____

seat

_____
_ _ _ _ _ _ _ _ _ _ _ _ _ _ _ _ _ _ _
_____

lawn

_____
_ _ _ _ _ _ _ _ _ _ _ _ _ _ _ _ _ _ _
_____

pants

_____
_ _ _ _ _ _ _ _ _ _ _ _ _ _ _ _ _ _ _
_____

tear

_____
_ _ _ _ _ _ _ _ _ _ _ _ _ _ _ _ _ _ _
_____

Directions In school, your child learned about synonyms, or words that have similar meanings. Read the words with your child. Have your child tell you which pairs of words describe each picture.

Name _____

Underline the word in the sentence that means the same as the word in the box.

1. | plate | Please put the <u>dish</u> on the table.

2. | hen | Sara has a pet <u>chicken</u>.

3. | also | I want to go <u>too</u>!

4. | city | We took a bus into the <u>town</u>.

5. | nap | Grandpa likes to <u>rest</u> in the afternoon.

6. | strong | A runner has <u>powerful</u> legs.

Vocabulary Lesson 17

Name _____

Read each sentence.
Circle the synonym of the underlined word.

1. We will <u>begin</u> class at noon.

   jump   laugh   start

2. The dog left <u>muddy</u> footprints on the floor.

   dirty   silly   cloudy

3. What was that loud <u>noise</u>?

   brush   sound   smell

4. The <u>sea</u> air was fresh and cool.

   ocean   garden   quiet

5. I want to <u>paste</u> this picture here.

   feel   keep   glue

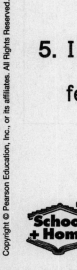

Directions In school, your child learned about synonyms, or words that have the same or almost the same meaning. Take turns reading the sentences with your child and ask him or her to tell you which words are synonyms.

Look up each word in a dictionary.
Draw a picture for each word.

window	house
tree	sheep

School + Home **Directions** Have your child look up the words in the dictionary and then illustrate them. Ask your child to tell you the meanings of the words.

Read the sentence.
Circle the correct definition.

The plane flew **over** the clouds.

over: at an end, finished
over: above, higher

Mom paid the **check.**

check: to look at something closely
check: a careful study

Frank uses his **trunk** to drink and pick up food.

trunk: the main part of a tree
trunk: a large stiff box
trunk: part of an elephant

Directions In school, your child learned how to use a dictionary to learn the meanings of multiple-meaning words. Read each sentence with your child. Then ask your child to tell you why the other meanings of the word do not fit in the sentence.

Name _____

Read the words and sentence.
Look up the words in a dictionary.
Fill in the right definition.

Word	Example Sentence	Definition
blossom	The tree will blossom in the spring.	
field	The detective was the best in her field.	
show	Can you please show me how to bake a cake?	
odd	The answer is an odd number.	

Directions In school, your child learned how to use a dictionary to find the definition and pronunciation of a word. Read the words and sentences aloud with your child. Then ask your child to look up the words in a dictionary to find the correct pronunciation and meaning. Help your child write the definition that makes sense in the sentence.

Name _____

Read the sentences.
Underline the definition of the bold word.

1. Today Jane is **absent,** or away, from school.

2. Who is your favorite **author,** or writer?

3. My cat **leaps,** or jumps, onto my bed.

4. The nurse will **aid,** or help, the sick boy.

5. Babies **bawl,** or cry, when they're hungry.

6. Who was the **champion,** or winner, of the game?

School + Home

Directions In school, your child learned how to figure out meanings of words by looking for definitions within each sentence. Read the sentences with your child. Ask your child to show you the definition of each bold word.

Read the sentences.
Circle the sentence that goes with the picture.

1. I ate a **pear** for breakfast.
   Dad has a **pair** of red socks.

2. Ann can **sew** a button onto a shirt.
   Because Joe was **so** tired,
   he quickly fell asleep.

3. We tied the rope into a **knot**.
   Josh did **not** eat the green beans
   because he doesn't like them.

4. I woke up when **I heard** a bird sing.
   We saw a **herd** of deer eating grass.

Directions In school, your child learned how to figure out meanings of words that sound the same by looking for clue words in sentences. Read the sentences with your child. Then ask your child to tell you the definitions of the bold words in sentences that are not circled.

Vocabulary Lesson 19

Name _____

Read the sentences.
Circle the words in the box that tell what the underlined word means.

1. The king was very angry. Nobody had ever <u>opposed</u> what he said or did until now. Everybody knew to keep quiet. Everybody knew to just follow his silly orders. But not this brave little girl! She had dared to speak up and say no!

written down	disagreed with

2. In the fall, Monarch butterflies in North America fly to warm places in California and Mexico. When spring returns, the butterflies return to lay eggs. Researchers <u>examine</u> butterflies to learn more about them. They take a close look at the paths butterflies travel.

move from one place to another	study carefully

School + Home

Directions In school, your child learned to figure out the meaning of an unfamiliar word by reading the words and sentences around it. Read the sentences with your child. Then take turns finding the clues that show the meanings of the underlined words.

Name _____

Read the words.
Group the cards.

help • ing	eat	eat • ing
look	help	look • ing
jump • ing	jump	

Directions In school, your child learned how to add the ending *-ing* to words. Read each word for your child. Then help him or her group the words. Your child may pair *-ing* words with their base words. He or she might also group *-ing* words together.

Vocabulary Lesson 20

Look at the pictures and read the words.
Add er or **est** to the base word.
Write the new word under the picture.

1.

tall _____

2.

young   younger

_____

3.

long _____   longest

 Directions In school, your child learned about the suffixes -er and -est. Read the words with your child. Then ask your child to show you what each word means.

Name _____

Read the bold words.
Write the base word on the line.
Read the sentence.

1. **Hopeful** means full of _____.

2. **Fearless** means without _____.

3. **Sleepless** means without _____.

Read the bold words.
Use one of the small words to finish the sentence.

1. A **bathroom** is a room with a _____.

2. A **snowball** is a ball made of _____.

3. The **weekend** comes at the end of the _____.

Directions In school, your child learned to look at word parts to figure out the meanings of words. Read each sentence with your child. Then take turns thinking of other sentences that include the bold words.

Vocabulary Lesson 20